*Emily,*

*Unleash Your Zebra.*

# SUCCEED

## LIKE A ZEBRA

*30 Ways to Achieve Success
in High School and Beyond*

**Nick Zizi**

ISBN: 9781981048663

**Disclaimer**

*At times in this book, I have tried to recreate events, locales, and conversations from my memories of them. In order to maintain their anonymity, in some instances I have changed the names of individuals and places. I may have changed some identifying characteristics and details, such as physical properties, occupations, and places of residence.*

R & Z Publishing

# NICK ZIZI
## UNLEASH YOUR ZEBRA ®

## DOWNLOAD THE ACTION GUIDE AND WATCH THE VIDEO SERIES FOR FREE!

**ONCE YOU LOVE THIS BOOK, WHICH I KNOW YOU WILL, PLEASE DO 3 THINGS FOR ME.**

1. Take a selfie of you with the book and post it on Social Media and tag *@NickZizi*

2. Leave us an Amazon Review even though you didn't buy it on Amazon.

3. Do a Facebook Live about your Top 3 insights from your book and tell your friends to get their copy at *www.Succeed LikeAZebraBook.com*

**Thanks in Advance and Congrats for Succeeding Like a Zebra!**

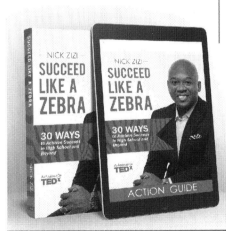

## WWW.NICKZIZI.COM/GIFT

This book is fondly dedicated to my wife, Sherline, and our five little zebras—Zach, Briana, Izzy, Eli, and Grace—who have been with me and supported me over the years while I have been traveling and speaking.

Also, I dedicate this book to my parents—Emmanuel and Marie—for always pushing me, and my sisters—Deborah and Daphne—for their belief in me. Without their support this project would have not been possible.

# TABLE OF CONTENTS

# INTRODUCTION
## *The Nick Zizi Zebra Way*

---

*A journey of a thousand leagues begins with a single step.*

—Confucius

---

ARE YOU READY to succeed like a zebra—in high school and beyond?

Do you want better results—in high school and beyond?

Would you like to land a great job—in high school and beyond?

High school is one of the most exciting and challenging times of your life. When you prepare yourself by maximizing every day, week, and month, then every lesson you learn will help build a strong foundation for your future. You can construct a springboard that will catapult you to greater success in college and the "real world" beyond.

In *Succeed Like a Zebra*, I am excited to share the thirty strategies proven to position you for maximum achievement. These are lessons I learned while I was a student like you in middle and high school, and also that I've gathered in my 15 years as a teacher, youth worker, and motivational speaker.

Because my strategies are compelling and relevant, I've shared them in talks at schools and conferences across the nation—including a TEDx conference in Jupiter, Florida. Because of the overwhelmingly positive response to my talks on student success and student leadership, I decided to compile everything into a single book, so middle and high school students everywhere have access to these standout strategies.

I am irrationally passionate about helping students just like you lead and succeed first on campus and then in life—and that's what you'll learn to do in the pages of *Succeed Like a Zebra*.

## Why a Zebra?

My name is Nick Zizi, and I study zebras. I've discovered that zebras are unique—no two zebras have the same stripes just like no two humans have the same exact strengths. We all are unique and gifted in our own way. When you find what I call your Z-print,™ meaning your special stuff, and you step out on it, you will stand out and be a stand-out success in life. So when I say, "Succeed like a zebra," I'm using the zebra as a metaphor for your uniqueness and maximizing your potential so that you can make an imprint at your school, in your community, and in the world.

## Who Is Nick Zizi?

In my first two years of high school, I was a bright kid who made the mistake of "following the crowd." That ended up getting me into a lot of trouble. My grades were not up to par because they were not my main focus. I tried to please and entertain my fellow students, trying to be the cool kid at any expense.

Once I started my junior year, I finally landed on the first big rule for success: in order for my life to change, in order for my future to be brighter, I must take responsibility for my life and actions ASAP (spoiler alert: this book ends with an exploration of this huge lesson!).

Next, I started writing down my goals, what I wanted for myself and for my future (spoiler alert #2—chapter 2 addresses this important practice!). As a result, things began to shift for me. As I began to enjoy the step-by-step achievement of my goals and the results of my hard work and careful planning, more options and opportunities opened for me. Success led to even more success.

In my quest to prepare for the future, I spoke to a lot of adults, asking for their best advice and guidance (spoiler alert #3: chapter 7 addresses this!), both in school and beyond. I remember speaking to Mrs. Haywood, one of my counselors. "I'm going to take a year off after high school, before going to college, because I want to take a break and figure things out. What do you think of that?" I asked her.

Mrs. Haywood replied without hesitation, "Nick, go to college immediately. You've got to keep your momentum going and not get sidetracked."

Her advice made sense. So, I joined a college jumpstart program, which allowed me to start college just two weeks after I graduated from high school. This early start was supposed to help students like me determine whether college was a good fit.

Fast-forward to a few years later: I earned three academic degrees. I'm running two companies as well as a leading nonprofit organization. I'm a philanthropist who provides scholarships to high school seniors in South Florida. And I'm a sought-after speaker on winning strategies for young people to enact to achieve top success.

I'm saying all of this to let you know that I got off to a slow start in high school. When I was a freshman and a sophomore, I got it wrong, but then I figured it out, made some serious changes, and catapulted myself on-track to where I had lots of options and opportunities. Because I've been on both sides of the coin as a high school student, I like to think I'm in a unique position to help all teenagers get it right. Plus, in my 15 years of teaching, mentoring, and speaking to teens, I've expanded my repertoire to include even more winning strategies, all of which I'm offering in *Succeed Like a Zebra.*

These strategies will help you to make your high school years the most enjoyable and exciting time of your life. You will learn how to:

- boost your grades,

- get the job that you want,

- win scholarships,

- improve your relationships with your friends, parents, and teachers,

- lead with confidence,

- craft a stellar resume,

- and so much more!

I guarantee that if you implement the strategies in this book, you—and those around you—will notice a major difference in your grades, attitude, and results. You will become enlightened, empowered, and invigorated. Fabulous options and opportunities will open for you. As long as you don't just read, but implement—take massive action—you'll enjoy these gigantic results.

## How to Use This Book

Most books are meant to be read. *Succeed Like a Zebra* was written to be used. I hope you will find the information in this book too valuable to simply glance over. By employing the strategies and ideas repeatedly, you will enjoy better and greater results throughout your high school years. Here is how I suggest you do this:

## First: Enjoy the Book

Have fun checking out the great quotes and zebra facts in each chapter. Be amazed and inspired at each chapter's personal stories, both from my own life and the lives of teens I've worked with. Skim through the pages at random; look for bits of advice that you can use immediately. Also, work on the exercises at the end of each chapter.

## Second: Find the Advice You Need

Review the table of contents for the strategies that will provide you the greatest value. Write a Z next to each chapter that holds the highest value for you. As you study the chapters (notice I did not say "read." I said "study"), take notes in the book. Underline key concepts, highlight what you want to remember, draw stars or circles. Make this book your own. Jot down any insights that will help you when you begin to apply the recommendations.

## Third: Set Priorities

Rank the titles in the table of contents that you have studied from most to least important and from most to least urgent. Identify the first one you want to work on.

## Fourth: Go to Work

Plan to spend your school year(s) working on these strategies.

- Some strategies can be completed in one go, and others need to be repeated over a period of time to get the results you desire.

- Turn to the page of your highest-ranked title, and write the date you want to begin it and the date you want to complete it.

- Next, study the chapter and get to work! Work on it until completion.

- If you can do two or three at a time, go for it.

- Make sure to work on the exercises too. You must do the thinking, reflecting, and writing indicated in the exercises to achieve the promised success.

- Finally, remember to enjoy it. This is you—your present, your future, your life—we're talking about it here, so enjoy it.

## Fifth: Sign Up for the "Succeed Like a Zebra" Mailing List

To further accelerate your success in school and beyond, sign up to receive additional support on a monthly basis through our emails, videos, bonus Q-and-A conference calls, events, and much more. Join Team Zebra today.

## Up Next

Now that you know how to use this book, it's time you get started. The first step in succeeding like a zebra—what chapter 1 is about—entails a notebook, a pen, and about 15 minutes of your time—today, tomorrow, and every day of the week.

# SECTION 1

## *Make a Plan*

Zebras don't wing it. They strategize to thrive in the wild. To thrive in school and life you must make a plan. In the first section of *Succeed Like a Zebra* you will learn how to make a plan by journaling, writing your goals, and finding what you are good at.

# CHAPTER 1

## *Write in Your Journal Daily*

*If your life's worth living, it's worth recording.*

—Tony Robbins

THE MOST SUCCESSFUL zebras in a dazzle (did you know that the word for a group of zebras is a "dazzle"? Yeah—fun fact!) have certain behaviors, things they do and don't do. For instance, they don't spend their time watching other zebras, concentrating on those other zebras' lives, dreams, and passions. No, the successful zebras in the dazzle take time each day to consider themselves and their dazzle as a whole— what they're doing, what they want to do, how they're doing, how they can best contribute to the dazzle, and more. They recall moments in their past and in the past of the dazzle, and try to learn from those times. The most successful of the most successful zebras do all this thinking, reviewing, and considering in their daily journal. Okay—admittedly, this isn't exactly accurate. But, bear with me—I'm trying to make a point!

Keep a daily journal. Why? Because your life is worth recording. When you record your life, you put yourself in the company of the greats and also you position yourself to make bigger achievements at an even faster rate than people who don't keep journals. Let me explain.

## In the Company of Greats

The late Helen Keller observed: "I don't want to live in a hand-me-down world of others' experiences. I want to write about me, my discoveries, my fears, my feelings, about me." What she means is that by writing a journal of her life, she's putting herself at the center of her life. She's immersing her energy, focus, hopes, and dreams into herself and her future—as opposed to getting sidetracked by reality TV stars, so-called friends on Facebook, and who's got the most "likes" on Instagram. Successful people put time and energy into bettering the world and themselves—and journaling is a way they do that. Join the company of great people and start journaling yourself.

My early mentor, the late great Jim Rohn, one of America's greatest business philosophers, said, "If you're serious about becoming a wealthy, powerful, sophisticated, healthy, influential, cultured, and unique individual, keep a journal."

All zebras journal. Zebras use this strategy to help them to succeed more. By keeping a journal you join the company of some famous zebras, such as Albert Einstein. Before his death in 1955, Albert Einstein bequeathed his entire literary estate to Hebrew University in Jerusalem, an institution he helped found in 1925. Among the 8,000 scientific and popular writings, drafts, lecture notes, and notebooks were also the famous physicist's travel diaries. Recorded between 1921 and 1933, they offer personal and amusing insights into Einstein's experiences traveling to places like Japan, Israel, and the United States.

You'll also be in great company with Mark Twain, aka Samuel Clemens, who wrote every day, journaling his life. Thomas Edison, the most productive inventor in American history, had over five million pages of notes in his entire lifetime, and most of them were journals where he jotted down his ideas as well as different experiences that he had during those times. Leonardo da Vinci also wrote in his journal. So many great zebras have written in their journals.

Oprah Winfrey, the television mogul, keeps a journal. She keeps a gratitude journal of the five things she is grateful for in her life that day. She regularly returns to past journal entries to see what it was that she was grateful for. There was this one time she reviewed an entry that she wrote many years ago. Here's that entry:

*Here's what I was grateful for on October 12, 1996:*

1. *A run around Florida's Fisher Island with a slight breeze that kept me cool.*

2. *Eating cold melon on a bench in the sun.*

3. *A long and hilarious chat with Gayle about her blind date with Mr. Potato Head.*

4. *Sorbet in a cone, so sweet that I literally licked my finger.*

5. *Maya Angelou calling to read me a new poem.*

In revisiting this entry, Oprah realized that she did not have the same gratitude sentiment towards those experiences today. She had gotten too busy. However, she reminded herself to look for the little things that in the past she'd been grateful for that now she was overlooking. She claims that keeping a gratitude journal has changed her life. Be a zebra like Oprah and keep a journal, so you too can reap big benefits and live a better life.

I remember many years ago when I was in elementary school, I learned about writing in a journal. As a child, frankly, I didn't see the importance of it. I thought it was fun to write about what happened over my weekend and it was an easy assignment, but I didn't understand the importance of journaling on a daily basis until after high school. That's when I was studying and reading many books, trying to figure out how successful people got successful. That's when I noticed that a lot of my mentors and the people that I looked up to journaled. I went and dug some more, did some research, and found that there were great benefits to journaling. That's when I became convinced that journaling would help accelerate the process of my success. So, because I too wanted to join the greats, I began journaling myself. Now, I've been keeping a daily journal for about 10 years.

## The Benefits

My goal in this first chapter is to get you to commit to keeping a daily journal too. The question, then, is—how does keeping a daily journal help you become great? Why does keeping a daily journal allow you to make greater achievements faster?

In keeping a daily journal, there's really two things going on—the writing of it and the rereading of previous entries. There are major benefits to both. For instance, writing regularly will improve your intelligence and communication skills. When you write, it also can serve as a mindful and meditative activity, meaning it will help you let go of stress and worry. The less time and energy you spend stressing and worrying means the more you have to think, act, and succeed. Also, writing something down increases your memory and understanding of it, which positions you to have a more mature and far-reaching perspective on your daily life. There is a healthy emotional release from journaling too.

I can remember one of my students that we will call Tiffany was writing while I was teaching a lesson. I asked her to sit up and pay attention to the lesson at hand, but within a few seconds she went back to writing in her journal. After class I asked her what was going on, and she told me that she had to write about how she was feeling to cope with her own depression. It was her way of relieving her stress. While writing during class wasn't ideal, I offered Tiffany as much support as I could, offering her space in my classroom to journal before or after class, because I agreed with her that journaling would benefit her greatly.

When you reread previous journal entries, you also reap amazing beneficial rewards. It's not uncommon for us to get stuck in ruts where we mistakenly believe we've made no progress in our lives and that we have a lot of problems. By revisiting previous journal entries—from weeks, months, or even years earlier—we have recorded evidence of how we used to be and how far we've come. It helps us realize we are in the driver's seat of our lives; we are deciders, not victims. It's empowering—and that's what I want for you too!

Robert kept a diary since he was in middle school. He would often review previous entries to see the lessons he had learned and the challenges he once faced. There was one entry where he was worried about new friends at his new school. He wrote about the fear of being rejected and being lonely. A few months later, he reviewed the entry and noticed that he was doing much better now and had good friends who had his best interest in mind. So he learned that many of the fears he had before were baseless and never happened. This realization has helped him realize his current fears were probably baseless too. He was able to put most of his focus on the positive.

Recently I reviewed some journal entries from a few months ago. I read about how I was frustrated because I had wasted valuable time watching movies on my Netflix app on my iPhone. I'd fallen in love with a new series, *The Flash*, and watched all of the episodes in a few days. It was that good. Seeing that it had been stealing the limited time I had, I ended up deleting the app (temporarily until I could gain enough will power to download it again and not binge watch!). Reviewing this entry helped me evaluate how I'd been spending my time since I'd deleted the app. Was I ready to get the app again? I decided that I wasn't. Not yet. Journaling gave me the power to make that decision.

## The What

The next question—what exactly is a journal? What are you supposed to write about? How do you keep a journal?

A journal is your personal record of occurrences, experiences, and reflections that you write on a regular basis. It can be a diary. It can be a notebook where you record many lists: list of life goals, list of books I've read this year, list of new words I've come across, list of colleges I want to apply to, list of inspiring quotations. A journal is a place to record your goals, advice, information, mistakes, lessons learned, and successes, all of which will build your self-confidence, help you identify areas in which you want to grow, and help you notice how you've grown and changed. A daily journal is a place where you come to know yourself better, so that you can make the best choices to live the kind of life you want to live. Keeping a journal allows you a tool so that you can identify your dreams and record your progress in achieving them.

## The Setup

How do you set up a journal? Let me share how I do it.

Currently, this is my go-to way of setting up my daily journal. I write every morning and evening for no more than 25 minutes per session. I set a timer for 25 minutes (you can do it for a shorter time period. The point is to focus just on journaling without any distractions). I set my phone on "do not disturb" during this time as well. On a given day, I divide my morning journaling into three sections:

## Section 1—Highlights from the previous day

Here's an example of a section 1 that I wrote four days ago:

*Yesterday was a good day. I taught on the importance of choosing the right friends to our students. The talent show was great. Amazing student performances. Trained leaders today and had a session on the importance of leadership. I told them that everything falls and rises on leadership, and that in order for things to change, they have to change. Also, received an email from a school that wants to bring me in to speak at their awards ceremony for their seniors in May.*

The reason I record these highlights is because my life is happening so fast that I can forget what happened in the past to make me who I am today.

## Section 2—My top five goals.

Here's an example of a section 2 that I wrote one day last year:

1. *Complete book outline*

2. *Exercise*

3. *Read for 30 minutes and take notes*

4. *Follow up with schools interested in the "Lead Like a Zebra" assembly program*

5. *Take kids to the park*

The reason I do this is because I want to focus only on the goals that are the most important to me. I can only hit a target I can see.

## Section 3—Three different lists

The first is a gratitude list of 5 things I'm grateful for in that moment in my life. The second is a list of the top 5 lessons I've learned that day. And the third is a list of the areas of improvements.

Here's an example of my gratitude list from a day last month:

- *I am grateful for my family.*

- *I am grateful for my health.*

- *I am grateful for a place to live.*

- *I am grateful for the opportunity to help students succeed.*

- *I am grateful for transportation.*

The reason I keep these lists is because writing down what I'm grateful for in the morning helps me to keep my mind on the positive and not on the negative that may occur during the day. Also, I write my top lessons learned from the day in the evening, so that I can remember and apply what I have learned for a longer period of time. When I review my list of areas of improvement, it helps me to come up with a way to get better in that area by writing it down and working on it the next day.

My use of these three sections and these lists has helped me tremendously. I return to the lists I've made—either a week, month, or year earlier, and I compare where I was at that time to where I am in the present. In this way I see how much I've grown in certain areas and how much I still want to grow in other areas.

## Zebra-Trail-to-Success Tips on Journaling

### *The Journal*

You don't need an expensive fancy journal. You can use a notebook—spiral, legal pad, sketchbook, whatever. You can purchase a notebook for $1 to upwards of $25 or more for a journal. Look for a good quality journal that will last during multiple uses. Keep in mind you will be using this notebook every day to record your life.

### *A Pen*

There are many recommendations for which pen to use for journaling. Here's mine: a Bic ballpoint pen. It is inexpensive, and you can get a box of 20 for just a few dollars. You may want to try different colors to match with a topic or section or mood. It's up to you. It's your journal.

The reason I believe in investing in an actual journal and pen—as opposed to using a computer or smartphone—is because with just a notebook and pen, I can concentrate. A computer or smartphone with its ads, notifications, and the temptation to surf the net is too much. I know that when I sit to write my entry it is in a journal and with a pen. No distractions. Also, writing with a pen instead of typing slows my thinking down, so I can actually analyze my thought process. But this is just me. You can record your journal on a computer or any other method. You have to do what works for you. Another option: writing in a journal and then scanning your entries into Evernote so that you will have the best of both worlds. You will have a hardcopy and a digital version of your journal.

## *Every Day*

Like I do, you need to carve out 15 minutes around a certain time every day that you'll journal—and commit to it. Maybe that means waking up 15 minutes earlier and journaling in bed. Also, morning journaling can be great because it focuses you for your day ahead. Maybe it makes more sense for you to journal after dinner each day at your dinner table. When I practice end-of-day journaling, it helps me reflect on my day's experiences and set goals for the next day based on them. The point is—don't just hope you can fit journaling into your day. You must carve out a time and place. Then, you must commit to actually doing it.

You can divide your journal into three sections like I did and make similar lists as well. Other ideas: write down your top five "lessons learned" each day or the top five ways you want to improve. You can return to these lists to evaluate your progress. If you write a list of areas that you want improvement in, you can review those at the start of the next day to help yourself avoid repeating mistakes.

Really, you can write whatever you want to write about in your journal. The point is to do it. To make it a habit. Over time, you'll find that this notebook that you've just invested in will serve as a great tool to help you to advance faster and farther in school and in life. Your journal will be the greatest book you've ever read because it's the book that you're writing. It's your life. It's your experiences. Your life is worth recording, so capture the moments by journaling every single day.

A great way to get into the habit of writing in your journal is to record all of your responses to this book's Zebra Action Time questions in your journal. This will kick start your journal habit, and you'll have a single place to look back at where you've recorded your responses. That's a nifty two-for-one!

## Zebra Action Time

1.  What are you going to write about in your journal?

2.  When and where are going to write each day?

3.  Why are you going to write? How do you think you'll particularly benefit from journaling?

This is important. If you're why is weak, you will not have enough motivation to write consistently. Take time on this one. You've read the chapter. Hopefully, I have convinced you by sharing the overwhelming benefits of journaling.

4.  If you run out of words or suffer from writer's block, try these three thought-provoking starters to get the juices flowing:

    *   Start writing about where you are that very moment. Describe your scenery, the time, the weather, your mood, etc.

    *   Write a letter to your younger/past self, starting: *Dear Past Me,*

    *   Write a letter to your older/future self, starting: *Dear Future Me,*

## Up Next

What goes hand-in-hand with the success you can achieve from keeping a daily journal? Writing down your goals. That's what we'll cover in the next chapter.

# CHAPTER 2

# *Write Down Your Goals*

*Success is the progressive realization of a worthy goal or ideal.*

—Earl Nightingale

ZEBRAS STRATEGIZE TO survive and thrive. In the African savanna, zebras will walk for miles searching for plains to graze, all the while staying together to protect one another from predators. In school and life, you will have to strategize to thrive. Goal setting is about working a strategy to live the life that you want. What do you want out of life? What type of lifestyle do you want to live? Which college or vocational school do you want to attend? The answers lie in this strategy: goal setting.

I was a little kid who failed kindergarten. That really troubled me, to the point that growing up, I felt that I was not smart enough. I knew that I wanted to graduate "on time," but I did not exactly know how I would accomplish that. Year after year, from elementary to middle school, I knew there had to be a way to skip a grade to make up for me having done kindergarten twice. As a freshman in high school, I met with one of my counselors who I then asked about the possibility of graduating a year earlier. He told me that I needed to meet a certain amount of credits for it to be possible. He advised that I take classes in night school and go to summer school.

So, I recorded my big goal: I will graduate a year earlier (to make up for having to repeat kindergarten). But that's not all I recorded because, really, that wouldn't have been enough. The big goal is the what; I also needed to write down the how—how I'd achieve that big goal. So, the next thing I did was record all the steps I had to take to achieve that goal. I recorded the classes, both during regular school hours, at night, and during summers, as well as the sequencing of the classes (because a lot of classes build off one another), I'd need to follow. I recorded how I'd have to divide up my few hours of free time when I wasn't taking classes so that I'd make good use of that time to do the study necessary to pass so many classes. Several years later—you guessed it—I graduated "on time," which, in my case, meant I completed high school in 3 years—all because I wrote down my big goal, as well as all the steps I'd have to follow to make it happen.

I have used goal setting to achieve greater success not just during my time in high school but also throughout college and professional career. It's just that powerful.

Notice from my own personal example that a goal isn't just a dream. Rather, a goal is a dream with a deadline. For instance, if your dream is to graduate from high school, the goal also includes the date you want to graduate.

## Gotta Write It Down

Why actually write down your goals? I know some people think, "I just don't have time to write my goals down. I'm too busy. I've got a lot of schoolwork to do, but don't worry—I know my goals. They're in my head."

The fact is that when you write down your goals, it helps you to focus and encourages you to work out the logistics required to make your goal materialize. Recording your goals in writing helps you to aim at a target in life, to live on purpose with purpose.

Researchers have done a lot of studies showing the amazing effect of writing down your goals. For instance, NPR reported on a study that Jordan Peterson at the University of Toronto conducted on the power of writing down goals. This study found that writing down goals nearly eliminated the gap in the dropout rate between all ethnic and gender groups at the Rotterdam School of Management. The students who wrote their goals were less likely to dropout of school.

Keep in mind—a goal in your head is dead. A goal on paper is alive. The written goal positions you to make it a part of your reality. Research repeatedly has proven that writing down your goals makes you significantly more likely to accomplish them. You are a thousand times more likely to accomplish a goal that you wrote down than the one you just have in your mind.

Let me give you another story—to really prove this point to you. This one is about a former student of mine. At the end of his sophomore year, when Jefferson hadn't passed either the FSA or the algebra EOC, in his junior year he determined he must make some goals and write them down. Jefferson told me, "I really panicked and started to doubt myself, but setting those primary goals really helped me focus on them. I'm currently a junior and I am ready to graduate because I took the time and set the graduation requirements as my goals for that school year. Now I can sit back and relax, and not really worry about anything except getting a job and going to college. That's what goal setting can do for you."

## The ZMART Way

What's the most effective way to do goal setting? Over the past fifteen years of speaking and coaching students across the nation, I have found the SMART goal-setting method to be the most effective. However, I've made a minor change to it. I call it the "ZMART" goal-setting method. Let's check it out.

### $Z$ = Zero In

The Z stands for "zero in." When making a goal, you must zero in on a target. In other words, your goals have to be specific. They can't be vague. What exactly do you want to achieve? Where? How? When? With whom? What are the conditions and limitations? Why do you want to reach this goal? What are possible alternative ways of achieving it? All of these are questions that you need to ask yourself when you're writing down your goals.

### M = Measurable

Your goals must be measurable, you must be able to track your progress and measure the level of success to be achieved. Your goal needs to answer questions, such as: How much? How many? How will I know when it is accomplished?

Let's say the goal is to graduate magna cum laude in your business major in four years. This is a measurable goal because it includes the precise level you want to achieve—magna cum laude. Also it entails the "by when" you want to achieve the goal; in this case, it's the day you graduate college in four years.

## A = *Attainable*

Is your goal attainable? That means you must investigate whether the goal is acceptable and even possible for you. You have to weigh the effort with the reward.

A lot of people say they want to start a business. For this goal to be attainable for you, you must determine whether it is something that you really want to do and whether it is something that you're willing to pay the price for. It may cost you 8 or 10 years to achieve. During that time when you will be working hard on that goal, there will be lots of struggle. So, you must determine whether it is something you really want for yourself. That's what's involved when making sure your goal is attainable.

## R = *Relevant*

Your goals should be important to you. Don't set goals because your friends or family want you to. Your goal has to be something that you want for yourself. Your desire for the goal will be the motivation you need to achieve it. So make sure it's your own. Also there are goals that may be irrelevant today that will be relevant a few years from now.

Imagine a high school freshman with this goal: *I want to be first in my class when I graduate from medical school.*

The problem with this goal is that it's not relevant to that high school student in this period of their life. It may be relevant in ten years, but more immediately, it's not. Why?

For one thing, they still have to graduate from high school. Next, they still must get into college and graduate from college. After that, they need to take a special test, the MCAT, to even be considered at medical schools.

Then, once they are in medical school, that's when that goal becomes relevant.

A relevant goal for the high school freshman would be this: *I want to have the best GPA out of all the freshmen every semester of ninth grade.*

## *T = Time-bound*

Make sure each goal has a specific timeframe for completion.

That goes back to what we said in the very beginning—a goal is a dream with a deadline. If it doesn't have a deadline, it's really not a goal; it's more of a wish. Set a timeframe for each goal. When do you want to achieve that goal?

Once you include a deadline, it will create a sense of urgency. It will create motivation. You'll feel motivated to work on it because you know that you're on the clock.

If you say, "I want to be successful, I just want to raise my grades in the next week, I want to raise them to all A+." That may not be an attainable goal if your current GPA is a 2.0 or a C. In fact in a week's time there is little that can be done to raise a grade by a whole letter. However, if you set out to bring up your grades for the next quarter and continue in that upward motion, then you set yourself with a reasonable timeframe to hit your target grade. So, make sure your goal is time-bound, and that the timeframe is reasonable as well.

What happens if you miss the deadline? Nothing. All you have to do is push the deadline back. In other words, let's say you set a goal to check off your list tomorrow. However, when tomorrow comes, you get bogged down with a lot of other priorities. What do you do? Change the end date to a later date. The point is to make sure you have a deadline, so even if you don't feel like you're going to hit the target on the deadline, you still try.

Let me give you another story—to show you just how effective the ZMART method of goal setting is. This one is about a former student of mine. Holly used the ZMART method to go to college as the first among her siblings. The pressure was on when she entered high school. Being the eldest and living at home with a single parent was a challenge that she had to endure. She knew that she wanted to go to college and help her mother with some of the expenses by getting a part-time job. Holly *zeroed in* on what she wanted: to go to college and help her mother with some expenses. Then she made it *measurable* by determining a way to track her progress: she broke down her goal into manageable milestones starting in ninth grade and going to college graduation. To determine if it was *attainable* Holly weighed the cost of time and energy it would take to achieve it and saw that, yes, it was possible. About *relevancy*: yes, it was very was important. *Time-bound*: she set her graduation dates. She graduated high school in 2017, and the date for her college graduation is June 2021.

## Zebra-Trail-to-Success Tips on Goal Setting

### *Display your goal where you'll see it every day.*

I have a huge calendar in front of me right now. It's a 30-day monthly planner. My objective for putting this on the wall is for me to write down my top goals for the month and also for the quarter. That keeps the goals in front of me—literally!—and helps me to stay focused on them, which makes it more likely that I'll achieve them. After all, I can't somehow forget my goals if they are staring at me every day.

## *Make it a marathon, not a sprint.*

Slow and steady is the way to pursue your goals. Think—hare over rabbit. Always work on your goals every single day—even if it's just a little bit. If you have just 10 minutes, allocate those 10 minutes to one of your goals. Ten minutes, seven days a week adds up—that's 70 minutes working towards your goal.

Think about it—say, you currently can run a mile in 11 minutes, and you want to do better. If your goal is to run an 8-minute mile by the end of the month, and you find that you only have 10 minutes to practice most days— then use those 10 minutes. Alternating a minute of slow jogging and a minute of all-out running for those 10 minutes will seriously increase your fitness level and prepare you to achieve your overall goal. You'll make more gains that way than if you practice once a week.

The takeaway: try to do something every day that will move the needle forward for you with all of your major goals.

By writing down your goals, you will enjoy not only long-term results but also short-term results. You can accelerate your success today by following the ZMART goal-setting method.

## Zebra Action Time

1.  You might want to record your goals and responses to the following in your journal—you know—the one you started after reading chapter 1!

2.  Write a list of ten goals that you would like to achieve in the next one to five years.

3. Write the number of weeks, months, or years it will take to accomplish each. For example, if you are a tenth grader in high school and one of your goals is to graduate from high school, then you have 2 years (and some months) to accomplish that.

4. Set a specific date for achieving each goal. Write the month, day, and year next to each one.

5. Break down each goal into pieces, from monthly to weekly to daily goals.

To do this: imagine a flight of stairs. Your goal is at the top, and you are at the bottom. What is the first step that you have to take to get to the next step? Set those steps as mini-goals or milestones that you can work towards on a monthly, weekly, and daily basis.

## Up Next

In writing down your goals you will need to consider what you are good at. That's what the next chapter is about.

# CHAPTER 3

## *Find Out What You Are Good At*

*Use what talents you possess; the woods would be very silent if no birds sang there except those that sang best.*

—Henry Van Dyke

IN THE WILD a zebra has to learn quickly what it is good at to survive. If a mountain zebra and a plains zebra swap places, they would not survive. The reason is a mountain zebra is a great climber. If you place it on the plains, it would not be able to fully use what it's good at. The same goes for a plains zebra. Finding what you are good at will help you succeed in a greater way like a zebra.

What does it mean to find out what you are good at? First, it means identifying what you already know you can do well and enjoy doing—and then getting better at that. Next, it involves immersing yourself in new experiences to find surprising new things you are good at that you probably didn't realize.

# Sharpen

A great way to find what you are good at is to hone the skills you already have. Spend time sharpening the saw. If you don't use it, you might lose it. Look for ways to use your skills daily to stay sharp. Also, push yourself to put yourself in a position to use your skills. You never know when an opportunity will present itself. Stay ready by honing your skills through practice.

If you are having trouble identifying your strengths and what you are good out, there are some great resources out there to help. There are a variety of personality tests that help people identify their strengths, which in turn can help them choose amazing career paths. One of the most common is the Briggs Myers personality test. Unofficial versions of it and information about the 16 personality types it provides are available on the Internet. You can take one of these unofficial versions to help you discover your personality type, so you will be in a better position to see from a general perspective what your strengths are or what you may be good at.

# Dig Deep

You don't know all the things you're good at until you try a lot of different things and really get out of your comfort zone.

Some people just don't try anything new because they are afraid that they will look stupid or clumsy. The fear of looking awkward or failing holds a lot of people back. One of the best ways to deal with the fear of failure is to consider the possibility that it might work out well and that you might like it. You want to try as many things as you can. Find what you are good at by trying new things.

For example, one of my former mentees Rebecca said this about finding what she was good at:

*When I was 16, I fell in love with movies. Yes, the cinematography was eye-catching, but I more so fell in love with the storytelling aspect of it. The way a film can capture an audience and control their emotions, I loved it. I began to take this new-found love seriously and started writing. I came up with a few stories but wanted to know more about filmmaking, so I decided I would attend film school.*

*In film school I learned a great deal regarding storytelling. My graduating class had to put together three different films created by us from start to finish. This meant first we needed stories. Everyone in the class was allowed to pitch an idea to the professors. I thought this would be a great opportunity to show what I could do. I wrote a story and prepared the greatest pitch I could come up with. I went into it alone. I stood there attempting to sell them this story. A story that I created. Coming out of my pitch with the professors, I doubted that I said the right words. I doubted that I did enough. I doubted that my story was good enough. A few days later we got the results. Out of all the stories pitched, mine was chosen as one of the top three. I felt excitement, surprise, fear, happiness, and so much more all at once. I found something I was good at, and it was something I loved. It's something I still love to this day.*

There are many benefits to finding what you are good at. You can get paid to do what you love, even if nobody is posting a full-time position for it. A Forbes article discusses how the economy is changing to dramatically increasing the number of people freelancing. A lot of people are doing what they love by freelancing. In 2015 a study indicated that nearly 54 million Americans are doing freelance work. If you're a good writer, as a freelancer you can write articles, blog posts, and do just about anything writing-related. The thing to do first is identify what you are good at, then practice to get even better, so you can reap the rewards, like getting paid to do freelance work involving that skill of yours.

Just as the zebra in the dazzle knows its strengths, so should you. Take a personality test to help you zero in on your strengths. Ask friends and family what they see as your strengths. Hone those skills you already know you possess. Try new things. You never know what you could excel at. Just be open to opportunities to try new things. Succeed like a zebra.

## Zebra Action Time

1.  Take an online personality test now. Google "Briggs Myers personality test" and take a quick test. I recommend recording your results in your journal.

2.  Ask those closest to you to tell you what they see as your strengths.

    As Les Brown pointed out, "You cannot see the picture when you are in the frame." Your parents, siblings, mentors, and closest friends may see some positive things about you that you have not seen or do not see. They will help you to pull out or wake up the zebra that is within you.

    - Make a list of the people you would like to ask.

    - Call or email your question to each person on the list.

3.  What comes with ease? What can you do easily? You will be surprised to see what comes up. Record it, and then choose one of those things to spend time developing more. Act on this.

4.  Make a list of five things you've never done that are out of your comfort zone but that you are interested, even a little bit, at trying out. Now, go for it. Try something on your list. Learn and get better.

Also record some things that you have tried but failed in that you still want to pursue. After that, make a plan to try them again.

5.  Would you like to consider freelancing? What type of work would you do? You can check upwork.com and fiverr.com to see how you can market your skills for an extra few hundred dollars doing what you are good it.


## Up Next

Finding what you are good at also entails developing your listening skills. Listen well to do well. That's what the next chapter is about!

# SECTION 2

## *Gain Knowledge*

To navigate the treacherous plains zebras have to be knowledgeable of where they are and where they want to go. To succeed you will need knowledge. In this section, we will cover the importance of reading, asking questions, becoming digitally literate, and more. You will gain the tools you need to navigate the plains of your education and life.

# CHAPTER 4

## *Develop Listening Skills*

---

*There is a difference between listening
and waiting for your turn to speak.*

—Simon Sinek

---

LISTEN LIKE A zebra. Zebras can spin their ears in any direction. The zebra listens for impending danger. It can adjust quickly to what is occurring in its surroundings. Listening can be the difference between life and death. It also can be the difference between success and failure. It is the one skill that is not directly taught in school but that you use daily. Developing it will make a world of a difference for you.

In my work with teens and adults for the past decade, I have discovered that most people are not good listeners. Most people are just concerned about what they have to say. It is a nuisance to speak to someone who cuts you off before you complete your statement. Relationships are negatively affected when one person doesn't listen. A child who doesn't listen to their parents will put a strain on the relationship. A student who doesn't know how to listen won't do well in school. You can miss out on a job because you failed to listen to what was being said. I am certain that you have, at one time or another, had an experience with someone who did not listen.

Also, you probably have not been the best listener at times yourself—I know this is something I still struggle with at times too!

I can remember as a teen when I struggled with listening to my parents. One time my mother told me about a certain friend of mine that she felt was a bad influence. She told me not to hang around that person. As she was telling me that I was interrupting her and telling her that she was just judging my friend based on what she saw. I continued to associate with the friend, and I got into trouble as a result of it. If only I had listened to my mother.

On the flip side, in algebra, I remember struggling with some of the concepts. Though I tried to get a grasp of things, it was really difficult. Once I became intentional about developing my listening skills during algebra class, paying close attention to the lessons and asking questions, I finally understood and then my grades got better too.

You will have to make a deliberate effort to improve your listening skills. It won't get better by just thinking about it, hoping, or ignoring it. You will have to work on it daily.

## Zebra-Trail-to-Success 7 Tips to Improving Your Listening

I've researched this topic for the past decade and have compiled some of the best tips from my personal experience and research. These 7 tips should be applied in conversations with adult "decision makers," meaning adults who can open doors for you. Yes, listening well will help with every conversation, but with adult "decision makers" it can make a huge difference. For example, if you are being interviewed for a summer job, you want to make sure you listen well.

## #1 *Win-Win*

Keep in mind that listening is win-win.

Too many people listen with a win-lose mentality, meaning listening with a closed mindset that says one of us will not come out of this conversation as a winner. "I'm right and you are wrong" or "My way or no way." You can never listen well with that mindset. Instead, hear the other person's view, hear what they're saying, and then if you have something you want to share, add to it. However, be sure to wait until they are done and then give it about 2 to 3 seconds before you say something. Why? Take this scenario—you're conversing with someone, you're just about to finish, and they have already started before you can take a breath. They are already answering your question. When this happens, it makes you feel unheard, like they were simply biding their time until you'd be quiet, so they could speak.

You don't want to do this to other people. You want to actually hear them. You want them to know you've heard them too. It will help you and them—that's why it's a win-win. So, give it about 2 or 3 seconds before you reply. Let their words sink in a little bit. Make sure you understand before you try to be understood.

## #2 *A Class Report*

Tell yourself that you will write a report about the conversation for class. Of course, you're not really going to do this, but by playing this scenario out when you listen, it reminds you to pay close attention to what the other person is saying. It reminds you to not assume you get it already—but to listen well to all their details, which will likely allow you to arrive at a deeper understanding than if you switched your mind off.

Pretending like you're expected to give a precise report, especially when you are being told something that's hard to hear, will help you engage with what's being said more deeply, so that you benefit more in the end.

## #3 *The Eyes*

Hold eye contact. Look the person in the eyes. Don't look at the floor. Don't look at their shoes. Don't look behind them. Don't shut your eyes— they may think you're falling asleep, meditating, or lost in your imagination, and just waiting for them to be quiet.

Eye contact is very, very important. You listen with your eyes. To avoid an awkward stare, look at their eyes for a few seconds, then the middle of the forehead close to the eyebrows for a second, then back to the eyes.

## #4 *No Phone*

Put your phone away. Put it down. You don't need to text or check social media. As a matter of fact, if you are playing on your phone because you think you are great at multitasking, research shows this simply isn't the case. It's an overestimation of your abilities. So, not only does your phone detract you from listening well, it also allows the person speaking to have a lousy impression of you. In order to go far in life, you need to make a good impression, and an easy way to do this is to never have your phone out when conversing with another person.

You should only use your phone if it is related to the conversation. The other day when I was talking with someone, I asked if I could take notes on what she was saying with my phone. The reason I asked was that I didn't want her to think that I was doing something else on my phone other than listening to her. Asking her and then taking notes also made a great impression.

When you focus on the person speaking, you make them feel better about you and about themselves. You make them feel heard. You can do that by simply putting your phone down while someone is conversing or speaking. Be there.

## #5 The Recap

Give a recap. Tell the person speaking to you what you heard them say, in your own words before giving your response. Why do this? For one, it shows them you are listening. But perhaps more importantly, you can help yourself and that person determine if your interpretation of their words is accurate, to ensure you're both on the same page. You will save everybody, particularly yourself, a lot of trouble by delivering a summary before you speak. When I do this, I typically start my response by saying, "Just to make sure I understand you, I'd like to give you a short recap of what I think you just said."

## #6 Note-Taking

Take notes if needed. When you are jotting down the key points in a conversation or lecture, it can really help you to listen better. Also, it makes you look good and makes the speaker happy because they feel heard. Even if you already know the information, by jotting down what comes to mind, you make an impression on the person speaking. They maybe will share even more important information with you. Note-taking isn't just something you do in a class or a presentation, it's great to do in one-on-one situations as well, like job interviews, college fairs, and college interviews.

## #7 *The Body*

Beyond just the eyes, really it's your whole body and posture that "listens" or appears to not be listening! Sit up. Lean forward. Nod when the speaker makes a statement that resonates with you. Show your engagement with your body and face. And the opposite is true as well—when you don't feel engaged, by going through the bodily "motions" as if you are engaged, then you can become so. Your physiology affects your state of mind. The way you sit affects how you listen. If you are feeling sluggish, sit up tall and keep close eye contact with a speaker, and it'll help you emerge from that tiredness. Think about a lion positioning itself to attack prey. Does it sit in a slouched way? No. It leans forward to be in a better mental and physical state to catch its dinner. Do the same. Change your physical state to be able to change your listening state.

In the beginning of the year, I had an engagement to speak at the Business Professionals of America State Conference, a national student leadership organization. I had two presentations that day on leadership. I remember a student by the name of Jake who was sitting in the front row of the conference room. Jake came to me after the session and asked advice on how to recruit more students into his club. When I began to tell him a few proven strategies to get more students interested, he took out a notebook and began to take notes. As I was speaking he kept eye contact and nodded his head. He made a striking impression on me that he was intently listening to what I had to share, which in turn encouraged me to share even more with him.

Once you begin developing these 7 listening skills, you'll be amazed at how your fellow zebras respond to you. Suddenly the leaders of the zebra dazzle will see you as one of them—a leading zebra. Sure, your ears don't have to spin, but you've got seven ways of your own to sharpen your listening prowess.

## Zebra Action Time

1. Of the 7 tips, which two do you know you already do well?

2. Of the 7 tips, which one do you know you struggle with? Even give the last time you know you messed up with it.

3. Make a plan of when, where, with whom, etc., you are going to be sure to change with that one difficult tip.

4. Next time you are in class put into action all 7 of these tips. Afterwards take notes on how the teacher responded to your obvious listening to them. Take notes too on the tips that were most difficult to enact. This will help you pinpoint the areas that need to be improved. After a short time of following this one exercise, you will enjoy amazing results.

## Up Next

Listening is a skill if developed that can make a world of a difference for you. Another such skill: reading. In the next chapter will we cover how reading like a zebra will help you stand out.

# CHAPTER 5

## *Read a Book a Week*

---

*It is what you read when you don't have to that
determines what you will be when you can't help it.*

—Oscar Wilde

---

IN THE AFRICAN savanna, although hot and dry, you will find zebras on the move, searching for greener plains to graze. A zebra relies on the daily consumption of grass, so that it can live. Just like the zebra, you cannot live without feeding your mind through reading on a daily basis. Read a book a week to succeed like a zebra.

Many fail to succeed because they don't read. Many fail to lead because they don't read. Many fail to raise their grades because they don't read. As you can see, there's a pattern here; not reading will keep failure ever-present. Watching a favorite movie doesn't compare to the amount of benefits you will get when you read.

When I graduated from high school and headed to college, I did not know what I wanted to do with my life. I knew I had to go to college, but I still felt very unclear about things. My father gave me the book *Think and Grow Rich* by Napoleon Hill. It was full of gems. Gems that I needed for clarity at that time. I learned that whatever I believe, I can conceive. I also learned that to change my life I needed to do it; no one else could but me. So, I went to college and worked at my family business—and the rest is history.

Today, because of that book and the hundreds of books I have read since, my life has changed for the better. I now am leading a non-profit organization and run two businesses. I am helping thousands through my radio show, keynote presentations, scholarship foundation, and the list goes on. I attribute my success and happiness to the many books I've read on a wide variety of topics.

I read books on student success, leadership, communication, goal setting, time management, and other topics. The primary books I read are non-fiction self-help books. I read books to learn something that I can apply to my life to make it better. While it is rare for me to read fiction, I'm sure I could learn from it as well.

There are many benefits from reading books. As you can see from my experience, it has tremendous value. Read—I can't encourage you enough!

## Some Benefits of Reading

- Expands your vocabulary

- Improves your writing

- Makes you smarter

- Reduces your stress

- Helps you to do better in school

- Develops your critical thinking skills

- Improves your focus and concentration

## Benefits Specific to Reading Fiction

- Inclusivity—stories open up your mind and connect you to distant people, places, cultures, and ideas

- Empathy—stories help you be a more understanding person.

You may be asking, "Why I should read one book a week?" My response: why not? If you can watch your favorite shows on demand or spend countless hours browsing online, you can read more than just one book per week. It's a challenge that I believe every teen can take on and do well in.

One non-fiction book may contain a year's worth of information. In some cases, decades worth of knowledge distilled into a hundred pages. I remember reading that one book has twenty or so books in it. The author researched other books and sources to write the book you are reading. The small investment you paid for the book cannot compare to the potential it has to change your life and make you a hundred times the investment.

People who read on a regular basis do better than those who don't. Students who read on a regular basis have a richer vocabulary, make more money, are happier, are in better relationships, and the list goes on. Reading on a weekly basis helps your mind to become sharper. You're able to sustain longer periods of reading and gain different perspectives that will help you to be a better communicator, leader, and all-around person.

According to research, after high school, the average American reads less than one nonfiction book per year. Let's say if you read one book per week, one book per week for a year, that's 52 books for the year. You would have a tremendous edge over your competition. It doesn't matter what field you're in. The more you read about your field, the more you will know. The more you read, the better prepared you will be to win in the marketplace. You can also read fiction books that are related to what you want to learn as well.

Guerdiana, a former mentee, told me, "Reading has always been a favorite hobby of mine. However, in middle school it became more like an escape. After being bullied for many months, getting lost in a good book was my way of coping. I spent so much time in the library that I won an award for the student who checked out the most books in the entire school! This experience not only increased my love for reading, but it also helped me to develop essential skills to succeed in my education journey."

## Zebra-Trail-to-Success Tips on Reading a Book a Week

### *Make it a habit.*

Read one book per week by setting a time and place every day to read. Set a daily appointment with your books to read. You can do this by allocating 15, 30, or 60 minutes a day to reading. For instance, you could wake 30 minutes early and spend the first 15 minutes reading and the second 15 minutes keeping your journal (remember, from chapter 1?). Or you could retire to bed 30 minutes earlier each night, and spend 15 minutes doing each. Just think, 15 minutes of reading a day adds up to almost 2 hours of reading each week. That really adds up.

## *Take advantage of those waiting moments.*

Read during your spare time—these are the short "gifts of time," as I like to call them, that we get throughout the day. You may be in a line, in a waiting room, sitting on the subway, etc. Instead of reading magazines or checking social media profiles, you could be reading a book. For you to do this, you have to have your book with you wherever you go. Maximize those 5- and 10-minute time gifts because they all add up.

## *Speed it up.*

Take a speed-reading course. I took a speed-reading course in college and it saved me because it taught me how to get through all the required readings from my courses. If you can go through the material faster, with greater retention, then you will free up more time. Fill in the blank with what you can do if you have more time.

## *Use the local library.*

Where can you find books to read? Good books? You can check your local library. It's free. Get a library card today if you don't have one, and make it a duty to use it often. Libraries also offer eBooks that you can rent. So you can access books on e-readers or use e-reading apps to read books off of your phone. That way, as long as you have your phone with you, you'll have your book too!

You can also find books at a local bookstore, and my favorite is finding books online. You can go to amazon.com and find tens of thousands of books. Also, there are places where you can get free books. Your school, library, and online are great places to find good free books.

## *Follow the tracks of great zebras.*

I like to see what other zebras are reading so that I can build my library. Let me give you a list of books that famous people like, so you can build your library following their tracks.

- Actor and dancer Zoë Saldana's favorite—*Lucy* by Jamaica Kinkaid.

- Barak Obama's favorite—*Song of Solomon* by Toni Morrison.

- Will Smith's favorite—*The Alchemist* by Paulo Coehlo.

- Steven Spielberg's favorite—*The Last of the Mohicans* by James Fenimore Cooper.

- Beyoncé's favorite—*Waiting to Exhale* by Terry McMillan.

- Actor and comedian Chevy Chase's favorite—*Moby Dick* by Herman Melville

- LeBron James's favorite—*The Hunger Games* Trilogy by Suzanne Collins

- The former Florida governor Jeb Bush's favorite—*Their Eyes Were Watching God* by Zora Neale Hurston

- Hillary Clinton's favorite—*Mom & Me & Mom* by Maya Angelou

Here's a list of books I recommend to teens looking to become zebras:

- *Think and Grow Rich* by Napoleon Hill

- *7 Habits of Highly Effective Teens* by Sean Covey

- *Success Principles for Teens* by Jack Canfield

- *Talent Isn't Everything* by John Maxwell

- *Living on the Edge* by Peter J. Daniels

You can also check a high school reading list for great book titles that many other students and educators recommend. You can ask adults and peers whom you admire and respect for their book recommendations. You can find out what the American Library Association recommends as a good starter list. Check out the Young Adult Library Services Association's (YASLA) teen book finder app. These lists will serve as a launching pad. Review the lists and mark the books you want to read.

Reading on a regular basis will change your life for the better. One book per month is a great place to start, but I want to challenge you, I want to raise the bar. I want to push you, and that's why I'm saying—read one book per week.


## Zebra Action Time

1. Make a list of the books you want to read.

2. Set aside a reading time and place every day. Your reading schedule has to be consistent. What time and where will you read every day? (Give yourself two weeks to build up to reading for at least 30 minutes a day.)

3. Set your weekly and monthly book reading schedule into your smartphone and a wall calendar that you can check off daily.

4. Take notes from your daily readings. Note the book's highlights, your favorite lines, and any lessons you may have learned. Also, include what you plan on implementing from the book that day and every day

of the week. Record those notes in your journal that you started after reading chapter 1 or save them in Evernote (or any similar software).

5.  Write in your journal about the results of applying the ideas from the book.

## Up Next

Listening is just as important as reading. Listening to inspirational and educational messages daily will condition your mind for success.

# CHAPTER 6

## *Listen to Inspirational and Educational Messages Daily*

---

*You are one message away from the life you desire.*

—Nick Zizi

---

ZEBRAS HAVE EXCELLENT hearing. They rely on what they hear to survive and thrive in the wild. The messages that you allow to enter your ears will determine your success. Thrive today by listening to inspirational and educational messages daily. Charlie "Tremendous" Jones said, "You will be the same person in five years as you are today except for the people you meet and the books you read." I would like to also add that you will become what you listen to. What you intake on a regular basis is determining your outtake.

I remember as a teen listening to Les Brown on cassette tape in my car going to and from school. The title of his message was "It Is Possible." I listened to that message every day. When I felt depressed because of a failed exam, I would hear the message in my head of how it is possible to come back after a loss. I knew it was possible for me to live my dreams. The message inspired me to keep going and reach for more. I want that for you too, so that's why I recommend: listen to inspirational and educational messages daily.

## TED *Talks*

One of the best ways to increase your knowledge is to listen to informational messages. TED Talks are known for having top-notch speakers on a wide variety of topics, including technology, culture, science, global issues, and design. Audio and video of TED Talks can be accessed through their free app. Listening to or watching a TED Talk every single day will help you tremendously because these are some of the best speakers in the world that share concentrated information in 18 minutes or less. In fact, I was privileged to have been featured in one of the TEDx conferences recently. Look up my TEDx talk to get motivated to "Unleash Your Zebra."

Jefferson, a junior, had to say this about TED Talks: "One TED talk I listened to was the one with Nick Vujicic. Nick inspired me because he had no hands, arms, or feet, but he didn't use that as an excuse for not succeeding. Nick talked about how rough it was growing up as a kid and a teen. He used to pray and wake up hoping he had hands and legs. He was really sad about himself at times, but he knew God had a purpose for him on this earth, so he didn't give up. He is able to do everything a regular human being can do. That really motivated me and gave me a strategy to rely on which is—never give up in any circumstance you're in because God has a purpose for you."

## *Podcasts*

Listening to podcasts will make you more informed, more thoughtful, and more connected to topics ranging from education, to leadership, politics, and sports. At EdTechReview you can find a list of 50 podcasts that are very relevant to high school and college students in the following categories: academic, general and special interest, entrepreneurship, and inspirational and motivational podcasts.

Here's a snapshot from that recommended list:

- 60 Seconds Health

- 60 Seconds Science

- A Way with Words

- Stuff You Should Know

- Talking Animals

- Tips and Tricks Photography

- Entrepreneurial Thought Leaders

- Founder's Talk

Carlos, a sophomore, enjoys listening to the *Stuff You Should Know* podcast. He said that it reminds him of those late-night study sessions, the ones that turn into people just talking about stuff. The show is entertaining and informative. He learns a lot of random facts, like how the pricing of gasoline works to how internships work. Also, he mentioned that most of what he has learned has helped him sound smarter because he's able to converse about many different topics.

Another great website that also has podcasts for high school and college students is collegeinfogeek.com. There's a great list of podcasts there as well that you can listen to every day. A snapshot of that site's list of 21 educational podcasts that will make you smarter includes the following:

- TED Talks (one of my favorites)

- RadioLab

- StarTalk Radio

- CollegeInfo Geek Podcast

- Back to Work

Many websites also host podcasts, so click around in your favorite websites to see if they have one. If you learn well when you listen to something (as opposed to seeing or doing something), then this is a great way to learn new information, i.e., by listening to inspirational or educational messages daily.


## *YouTube University*

YouTube is one of the best resources online. I call it YouTube university. You can learn just about anything there, from study hacks to relationships/dating advice to technology to applying for a scholarship to running a business. You can also search for inspirational messages to keep you motivated while you study. For instance, you can hear talks, speeches, and performances by amazing folks like Dwayne Johnson, Olympia LePoint, Denzel Washington, Eric Thomas, Michelle Obama, Prince EA, and Ashton Kutcher.

## *Nickzizi.com*

Another great resource for you is my website, nickzizi.com. There you will find dozens of videos on various topics including leadership, studying, communication, and motivation. My short, content-filled video messages will help accelerate your success.

I don't want to limit you to only podcasts and YouTube. You can listen to whatever falls under the categories of inspirational and educational. Audiobooks, documentaries, movies, music—whatever, as long as you are interested in it and you learn something. You can listen to audiobooks on your way to school.

To succeed like a zebra you will need to listen to inspirational or educational messages daily. Your survival depends on what you listen to the most. Thrive today by listening to positive, uplifting inspirational and educational messages that will help you unleash your zebra!

## Zebra Action Time

1.  Carve time in your calendar to listen to inspirational or educational messages daily. What time will you listen during the day? Will you listen while you are commuting, exercising, cleaning, or waiting in line? Do it today. Deliberate effort trumps intention.

2.  Make a list of the programs that you will listen to. Write the title of the program that you will be listening to every day of the week into your calendar. Also include what you plan to listen to this week. Review this chapter for ideas.

3.  Do this while listening: take notes, ask questions, and implement the ideas. You can record your notes right in that calendar entry where you

reminded yourself of the scheduled program. When taking notes, only record what resonates with you. Ask questions to go deeper and for clarification.

## Up Next

In addition to listening to incredible programs, asking your parents for their best advice will help you get the most out of life.

# CHAPTER 7

## *Ask Your Parents or Guardians for Their Best Advice*

*Your parents or guardians have a wealth of knowledge that you can learn from. If you don't, you may pay a hefty price learning the hard way.*

—Nick Zizi

A BABY ZEBRA, called a foal, follows its mother closely throughout its first year, observing which flora to consume. The foal learns by observing its parents. Imagine for a moment if the foal thought it already knew all there was to life. It would not last long. The seventh thing that you need to do before you graduate from high school is to ask your parents or guardians for their best advice. Believe it or not, your parents or guardians know more than you do. They have experienced a whole lot more than you have in the few years you have been here. So, take the time to learn from them.

I can hear you saying that your parents already give you advice without you asking for it. I get it. There are times you may wish they did not give you so much advice.

Okay, what if I told you that asking specifically for advice in an area of your life that you need guidance on will help you win more significantly in life? There's so much you can learn from your parents. Neglecting the opportunity to ask for advice robs you of all that is possible.

At times it may seem like parents or guardians are out of touch or even old-fashioned. However, their experiences will serve as a goldmine if you know how to extract the value. I learned all this late. I waited until I was in my early twenties to intentionally ask my parents for their best advice. Sure, they shared directly and indirectly lots of advice while I was growing up, but it wasn't the same as if I'd intentionally asked, "Dad, can you give me your best tips for school? Can you give me your best tips for college?"

It was during the time I was courting my then-girlfriend who later became my wife that I intentionally asked my parents, "How do I know if she is the right person for me?" My relationship with her was new for me. I had never gone that far in any of my previous relationships. I did not know whether I should marry her.

After speaking with my parents and asking for advice, I was able to glean years of wisdom in a few minutes of conversing with them. My parents told me that marriage is a serious bond and that everything should be considered when making a decision. They also mentioned that when you marry, you're not just marrying the person but the family. They said to consider her upbringing and family too.

I am so glad that I did. My wife and I are happily married with five little kids, including the new addition that arrived at the time of writing this book. My parent's advice helped me make the best decision of my life.

Once I realized the value in asking my parents intentional advice questions, they shared valuable insights about the questions I asked concerning friends, school, business, relationships, finances, and more. The insights that I learned just by asking questions have helped me to become the man that I am today.

When you ask your parents or guardians questions and they give you their insights, it's going to shorten your learning curve. Your parents know a lot more than you do. Sometimes they'll share information with you that took them years to learn, and they're giving it to you for a fraction of that time. You don't have to pay anything for it. You just have to take heed of the advice, so that you won't repeat the same mistakes that they made. That's a tremendous value right there. Your parents, your guardians, are a tremendous resource, so take advantage of the relationship by asking for advice.

Something equally important is to make sure you ask your parents to teach you particular skills before you leave home to start your life as an adult. On collegeraptor.com I came across the article "Five Important Skills You Should Learn from Your Parents Before College." Here are those five skills:

- *How to do laundry*—believe it or not, you don't just throw everything into the machine. Not only that, it's more than just separating white and colors. So, go ahead and ask your parents to teach you the tips and tricks of doing laundry the right way.

- *How to manage money*—avoid being the average broke college student by learning how to create a budget and live on it.

- *How to feed yourself*—you don't want to eat out all the time. After all, it'll certainly get expensive, and it's usually not the healthiest thing to do either. Ask the cook in your family to teach you how to prepare those key dishes.

- *How to plan and schedule*—set the course of your day by knowing what you will do in every hour of the day. Ask your mom, dad, or guardian about their scheduling.

- *How to read a map*—learn how to read a map, whether it's a hardcopy or on your phone. You never know when you may need to know how to get around especially when your GPS is not connecting to the network.

A few skills I want to add to that list include asking your parents or guardians the following:

- *How to clean a house*—you will need to know how to dust, mop, sweep, and everything in between to maintain your space.

- *How to jump start a car and replace a flat tire*—you want to be prepared for anything that can happen to your means of transportation: your vehicle. Go ahead and ask!

- *How to know when to service your car*—not knowing when and how to service your car can cost you hundreds to thousands of dollars that you could have saved had you known. Ask a parent or guardian how they determine this.

- *How to negotiate unfair situations at work or deal with difficult colleagues*—conflict resolution skills are vital to succeeding with people. I imagine your parent or guardian has a lot to share on this issue!

There's so much that parents do that we may be so used to that we don't think about—until we're suddenly living on our own. Take the time now when you have adequate time to learn and practice to ask your parent or guardian to teach you these life skills.

## How to Approach Your Parents

Broaching best advice conversations with your parents, especially if you've vocally resisted their unsolicited advice, can be difficult. Teen Health suggests that you start with small talk before you get into the big talk. When you approach your parents, you want to make it as smooth as possible. It's like walking into a pool instead of diving in. You do that by talking about everyday stuff a little bit each day for several days. You can talk about school stuff, sports stuff, something strange or funny you learned on social media—it doesn't matter. The point is to build a bond by talking to your parents daily. Once you've done that, then it's easier to bring up the big topics.

## How to Talk So They Will Listen

If you want your parents to listen to you, heed Teen Health's advice:

1.  Be clear and direct.

2.  Be honest.

3.  Try to understand their point of view.

4.  Try not to argue or whine.

To get the most from your conversations with your parents use these steps as guideposts to help you through the process. Also, review the chapter on listening to make sure you practice great listening strategies during these conversations.

Life is short. We don't know how much time we have left. Oftentimes we may think that we will get to do something several years down the line. In the context of this chapter, you may feel as though you may have time to ask your parents questions when you are older. Don't wait. Ask your parents questions about their youth and what they would do differently. Ask your parents about their biggest failures. Ask your parents about their friends when they were teenagers. Get best advice from them now.

There is so much to learn. So many experiences. So many lessons. You won't have time to go through it all. However, you can learn from your parents. You can shorten your learning curve. You can accelerate your success. You can reduce the number of times you bump your head, figuratively speaking. You don't have to try on your own. You can ask your parents specific questions to get meaningful insights. Start today.

## Zebra Action Time

1. What topics would you like advice on from your parents or guardians?

2. Write questions based on the topics.

3. Which category(s) are your questions in? For example, is your question related to school? If yes, then it would be in the education category. If you have a question on relationships, that would be in the relationship category.

4. Record your questions in categories in your journal.

5. Consider asking: if you could relive being a teenager again, what would you do differently? What area of my life do you think I need to improve in the most?

## Up Next

Just like parents, mentors can help you in a tremendous way by giving you advice and challenging you to reach higher. In the next chapter, I'm going to challenge you to find a mentor.

# CHAPTER 8

## *Find Mentors*

---

*A mentor is someone who sees more talent and ability within you than you see in yourself, and helps bring it out of you.*

—Bob Proctor

---

ALL OF THE great zebras that I have studied had mentors. Jordan, Obama, Mandela, and Gandhi had mentors. Students who have mentors accelerate their success. Be a zebra and look for mentors. Dr. Mike Murdock said, "The quickest way to success is through mentorship." Mentorship expedites your success. In fact, studies show that people with mentors are more likely to succeed. Look for mentors today to help you accelerate your success in school and life.

When Michael Jordan was recruited by North Carolina, his life changed for the better. His coach Dean Smith helped him hone his skills on court and off. Jordan recounts a time when Smith told him as a freshman not to heed the advice of people encouraging him to buy a restaurant. Jordan knew then that Coach Smith was not just interested in his ability to play the sport but in him as a person. When Jordan was asked about Coach Smith's impact on his life, he said, "Other than my parents, no one had a bigger influence on my life than Coach Smith. He was more than a coach—he was my mentor, my teacher, my second father. Coach was always there for me whenever I needed him and I loved him for it. In teaching me the game of basketball, he taught me about life."

As a freshmen in college, Mr. Roberts, my business lab instructor, played a vital role in the direction I would take. I would go to lab nearly every day of the week to work on my accounting assignments. One day I asked for assistance on the different types of statements. After he explained what each one was and how I could use it, he asked me questions about what I wanted to do with my business degree. I told him that getting my degree was not a top priority for me and that I was going to focus on the family business instead. He told me that would be one of the biggest mistakes I could make. He also said that I needed to complete my degree and then I could build an empire. I'm glad I heeded his advice.

A mentor is someone who has greater experience and knowledge in a particular area than you and who is willing to teach you the ropes. This can include experience in a particular job or career, in a particular college or academic study, in a particular hobby or sport, or even an all-around "how to be a good person and live a successful life" kind of mentor.

With a mentor helping you, you don't have to endure the same challenges that they had to go through to learn. You can learn from their experiences. Also, your personal connection to them can open up amazing opportunities for you. Your mentor's connections to certain people, events, programs, and skills could make all the difference in you getting into a certain college, landing that amazing scholarship, or getting through the first round of interviews for a particular job or internship.

# The Role of Your Goals

You can't land a good mentor until you know exactly what you want. This takes us back to chapters 2 and 3: identifying and writing down your goals as well as determining what you are good at. Once you've done that, then you are best positioned to know the kind of person or kind of skills and knowledge the person should have to be an effective mentor.

When your goals are clear, then you can move on to identifying your mentor. There has to be a selection process. You are not the only one doing the choosing here. Your chosen person will also have to decide if they want to be your mentor. It has to be win-win.

If you are wondering, "How can it be a win-win? What does a mentor get out of it?" then consider that working with you allows them to stretch their knowledge and skills. Also, they can expand their legacy by having you as a protégé. As a mentor to several teens myself, I also know there's great satisfaction in giving back to young people in the same way that mentors helped me when I was their age.

# The Where

The question to ask now is "Where can I find mentors?" Good question. You can find them in many different places. Start at home. Your parents or guardians would be the best place to start. Second, you can search for mentors at school, your school faculty. In an article in *US News* Dr. Brian Witte shared three individuals you can turn to for high school mentorship:

- *A teacher in a favorite subject*: your teacher in most cases has real-world experience and can help you navigate the uncharted waters of college and beyond.

- *An extracurricular leader*: great mentors don't have to have deep knowledge of your intended career field. A mentor can be anyone who wants to help you succeed. At your school, it can be your coach or music teacher.

- *A community leader*: you will have to branch out of school to find these people. It may come through volunteering or working a part-time job. These people can also include family members who have done what you want to do.

Your school may offer formal mentorship programs that you can join. I can't recommend it enough for you to look into these because I benefited from one of these when I was in high school. My high school's formal mentorship program, called 500 Role Models, connected us students to leaders in the community who gave us guidelines on how to be successful and responsible. For example, Mr. Merriam taught me how developing leadership skills could help me succeed in the business world, and Mr. Williams taught me about the importance of dressing for success. Many of the mentors I had through that program might have never crossed my path if I'd tried to reach out to them personally.

## Keeping It a Win-Win

I've mentored dozens of students over the years. The students who stand out are the ones who follow through with my advice and do all they can to be helpful to me as well.

Of course, there were a few students too who stood out in a negative way. There was one whom we will call James who started out well. He would take notes and show that he was applying what I shared with him. Later, he became very cocky and felt like he did not need any advice. He even went as far as leaving school early. His bad attitude prevented him from getting more help from me.

Here are a few ways to avoid being a "James" and to ensure you have a good relationship with your mentor:

- Respect your mentor's time. If you want to meet or talk on the phone, give them a timeframe as well as the particular topic you want to discuss. For example, "I was hoping I could stop by your office for a 20-minute talk about what you recommend I do to prepare for my college interview. When is a good time for you to do this?"

- If you have routinely scheduled calls or get-togethers, always be prepared. Don't just show up and expect them to lead things. Instead, have a list of topics and questions that you hope to be addressed.

- Look for ways to be of service to them. For example, if they have meetings, then volunteer to help at those meetings. You could pass out documents or help attendees sign in. If you find an article that addresses an area of their interest, send it to them.

One of the things that will make your mentor the happiest and willing to share even more with you is to see you implementing what they've shared with you. The best compliment you can give your mentor is to actually do what they are telling you to do. Show your mentor that you have implemented the advice they've shared with you. For example, if they've talked to you about the importance of always writing thank-you notes to important people who have given you their time, then send them a thank-you note. If they've suggested an amazing podcast or mentioned a newspaper article that they think you'd like, then send them an email mentioning something that you heard or read in that podcast or article that you found really interesting. This way you are showing them that you are using their insights.

As long as you do what it takes on your end to show your mentor respect, then the mentorship can help accelerate your success. A mentor will stretch you. They will push you to greater heights. They will bring out the zebra in you.

## Zebra Action Time

1. What are your goals as it relates to mentorship? Why do you think you need a mentor?

2. Write a list of names of people you would like as mentors and write down one specific lesson you would like to learn from each.

3. Distill your list down to one mentor. Who would that person be? Make sure it is someone you can reach out to today via phone, email, or face-to-face.

4. Start the process of reaching out to that one mentor. Call, text, or meet the person by asking a simple question, "I would like to learn from you. Can we talk about the possibility of you becoming my mentor?"

5. How and in what ways can you add value to them? Write at least five different ways you can help them out. These are things you can mention in the conversation with them about the possibility of a mentorship.

After establishing a strong mentor relationship with this person, you may want to repeat steps 1 through 5 for others on your list to have additional mentorships.

## Up Next

Your teachers and counselors can be great mentors too. What we'll be discussing in the next chapter: how to reduce the stress associated with the college process by asking your teachers and school counselor for college advice.

# CHAPTER 9

## *Ask Your Teachers and Counselors for College Advice*

*In life, you need many more things besides talent.*
*Things like good advice and common sense.*

—Oscar Wilde

F A ZEBRA tries to go at it alone without seeking advice from the experienced zebras in the group, it may lose its life. Don't let that happen to you. Ask your teachers and counselors for college advice.

As a teacher of middle and high schoolers, I know firsthand that my job is not limited to what's in the textbook. It's also my duty—and mission—to help my students apply what they are learning in class and beyond. My overall aim is to help students succeed in my classroom and also in life. That's why I came to teaching, and it's why most teachers choose the profession. For this reason, teachers will welcome you to talk to them about applying to college, going to college, paying for college, choosing a college major, and such.

Will, one of my mentees, shared this about asking for advice on the college admissions process: "I remember asking my career advisor about the many colleges that I could apply to and she suggested that I go to a college fair. At the college fair I was able to pick five colleges, but also hold Miami Dade College as an option if I had no money. I had no money, so I ended up going to Miami Dade College, where I earned an associate's degree. From there, I went on to Barry University, where I'll be graduating very soon, in just five weeks, with a bachelor's in biology and sociology. I'm so glad I talked to my career advisor when I was in high school. She helped me figure out a plan for college based on my financial situation."

Don't wait until your senior year of high school to start thinking about college. Start talking to your teachers and your school counselor today—as a middle school or high school student in any year.

Your teachers and counselors are in the best position to help you. They are trained and willing to help you navigate the process. They also have access to resources that will make the application process to college or vocational school easier. They can help by proofreading your applications and essays. Colleges ask that teachers write you letters of reference, so you can ask them to do this too. They can also help you sign up for admissions tests, like the SAT, SAT II, and ACT.

Asking for their advice will shorten your learning curve. You don't have to spend countless hours researching online or throwing money away investing in the wrong courses. To prevent that from happening, consult with them early.

## Prep for the Conversation

Ask your teachers if you could do a short interview with them about their tips for college. Beforehand, write down all the questions you want to ask, so you come prepared. You can even send them your questions ahead of time so that they can prep. You can ask questions about your educational strengths, about recommended majors, colleges, and financial resources. Moreover, you can ask about what it takes to get into your top choice of college. Make a list of your top questions to ask.

Be sure to ask for their permission to record the conversation as well. You will get everything when you record it. Consider taking notes during the conversation as well.

There's one other benefit that needs to be emphasized. When you implement this strategy, it will put you in a better position to get an excellent recommendation letter from your teacher or counselor. Why? Because they will see that you are a serious, forward-thinking young person with goals and dreams that you are determined to make happen.

Ask your teachers and counselors for college advice, which will make it easier for you to plan and transition into college or vocational school. Your teachers and counselors are trained and willing to help you with your questions. All you have to do is follow the simple steps laid out in this chapter to get the ball rolling. You will shorten your learning curve and speed up your success, just like a zebra.

## Zebra Action Time

1. Make a list of all of your teachers and counselors whom you'd like to speak to about college.

2. Write out your most pressing questions about school and college.

3. Ask your teachers/counselor(s) about a good time to do a short interview. Set the date. Come prepared. Ask your questions.

4.  Verify the information you're given. If it fits with your overall college goal, proceed.

5.  Gather your notes from all of your interviews. Categorize. Prioritize. That is to say, place the key topics in a category, subtopics in another category, then prioritize the notes.

6.  What are the steps you plan to take to help you achieve your goal? What is step one? The advice you will hear will push you further, but you must figure out what the steps are. Steps help break down big complex goals into manageable chunks that are easier to execute. You may want to start with the desired result. For example, it could be graduating at the top of your class four years from now. All you would have to do is work your way backward from the moment you receive the degree to where you are now. What are the steps you would have to take to get there?

## Up Next

A teacher's advice can shorten your learning curve just as learning to play an instrument can make you smarter, something you'll learn more about in chapter 10.

# CHAPTER 10

## *Learn to Play an Instrument*

*It's easy to play any musical instrument:
all you have to do is touch the right key at the
right time, and the instrument will play itself.*

—Johannes Sebastian Bach

S OME OF THE greatest minds in history were zebra musicians. Among the kings of Baroque music, Beethoven, Mozart, and Bach are the zebras that come to mind.

One of the great skills that I learned at a young age was learning how to play an instrument. I learned how to play the trumpet at the age of 13. It was challenging. There were times I felt like giving up. But I'm happy that I continued through the process. I joined the school band. In high school, I also played in the band and continued to master the instrument. I still play the trumpet to this day.

It's been over 15 years since I first started playing the trumpet in middle school. What I personally enjoy about it is its sound. I most enjoy it when I get the chance to play with other musicians who stretch me to become better. In school I enjoyed the friendships that I had with fellow band members. I also enjoyed playing at the various school events. Currently, I enjoy the challenge of keeping up with younger musicians in my church band.

Research has shown there are multiple benefits to learning to play an instrument, including improving and increasing memory. It also helps teach perseverance. It enhances hand-eye coordination. It improves reading skills. It also encourages self-expression.

Here's another great benefit that I like a lot. It makes you smarter. In fact, there was a study where researchers found that people who played an instrument do a lot better in their academics than those who do not. The reason why is that the parts of the brain that control motor skills, hearing, storing audio information, and memory become larger and more active when a person learns how to play an instrument. With these parts of the brain larger and more active, other parts of the person's life not directly related to the instrument improve as well, such as greater alertness, an increased ability to plan, and greater emotional perception.

Another great benefit of learning how to play an instrument is it improves your social life. It helps you to connect with other musicians. We're living in a time right now where we're just glued to our phones and social media profiles. A result is that we are very disconnected from others. Instead of talking to the person next to us, we rather text the person next to us. When you play an instrument, it helps you to improve your social skills. When playing in a band, you have to communicate with those around you, in real time, to play in harmony.

There are several other great benefits that you will enjoy as well from playing an instrument. It relieves stress. Whenever you feel stressed out with tests and the demands of school, when you play your musical instrument, it helps to relieve the stress.

One of my mentees, Kenny said this about learning to play an instrument: "When I first started high school, I was very introverted and timid. After trying out for different clubs and never really fitting in anywhere, a buddy invited me to practice in his band. He started to teach me how to play the trumpet. I always loved music, but learning to read and play music took my love for music to another level. Learning to read music was like learning another language, but I grasped the concept quickly. After a year and over 1,500 hours of practice, I became good enough to play along with my music teachers and even compete with other trumpet players and instrumentalists. Before I knew it, I began to shed my cloak of timidity and make more friends than I ever had."

If you perform in recitals before people, it gives you valuable experience being before a crowd. You could use this experience to develop your public persona skills and to help you handle any nervousness you may feel as well.

Maybe you are thinking, "Nick, I'm just too old. I'm in high school now." Well, let's say you start now. You join the band. You take a music class, and you learn an instrument. It's not too late because you'll be in high school for several years. If you go to music or band class and practice over a year or more, then you can learn a lot and start enjoying the many benefits music provides. Don't wait until later. You may not have time. Do this today.

If you are asking, "Nick, how do I do this? How do I learn how to play an instrument?" One of the easiest ways is to take a music class at your school. Secondly, join the school band. You may not be able to purchase an instrument right now, and that's okay because schools have instruments that they'll allow you to use during the time that you're taking the class or playing in the band. You can also look online for used instruments for sale at great prices.

Some instruments to consider learning to play—some known and others less so—include: trumpet, ukulele, bass guitar, French horn, and the piano.

Once you've started learning how to play, you want to practice on a regular basis. Ask your music teacher or band director for some tips that will help you to practice on a regular basis so that you can improve your playing.

Learning to play an instrument may seem optional, but the benefits are not. Increase your chances of succeeding on a higher level in school and life by learning to play an instrument.

## Zebra Action Time

1. Who is your favorite musician and why?

2. Which instrument would you like to play?

3. What do you like about the instrument?

4. When do you plan to start? Sign up for music class. Join the band.

5. Set your daily practice schedule. Plan ahead to keep the momentum.

## Up Next

Playing an instrument is a skill that will make a big difference in your life. Mastering the skills you learn in school, the focus of the next chapter, will help prepare you for a more successful college or vocational school career.

# CHAPTER 11

## *Master the Skills You Learn in School*

*It is possible to fly without motors,
but not without knowledge and skill.*

—Wilbur Wright

ZEBRAS MASTER THE skills that they have learned while in "school." A foal learns to walk and run with the dazzle in the first fifteen minutes after birth. It masters the skill long after learning it. You can too.

I remember reading an article about one of the greatest basketball players of all time, Michael Jordan, that addressed his dominance in the NBA. It was not the fancy moves or the length of time he was in the air, but the basics—dribbling, layups, jump shots, and free throws—that Jordan practiced to mastery level. As a result, he was able to make incredible shots due to mastering the basics. The lesson here is that mastering the basic skills you learn in school will help you do great in college and beyond.

The Bureau of Labor Statistics shows that median weekly income rises and unemployment rate drops with level of education. The unemployment line can be shorter when students like you see the importance of acquiring and mastering the skills that you are learning in high school. Do not do just enough to pass tests, but master the skills that you're learning because you're going to need them in college and beyond.

The SAT and the ACT, the two standardized tests used in college admissions, have benchmark scores they use to determine if test-takers are prepared for college. According to the ACT, 64% met the English benchmark, 46% of students met the reading benchmark, 38% met the science benchmark, 28% met all four benchmarks, and 31% met no benchmarks. According to the SAT, 41% met the benchmark. These tests measure skills that you have learned while in high school. Make sure that you master the skills so that you pass these tests and have more options in terms of college admissions.

## Those Other Crucial Skills

In addition to mastering subject matter, you are also learning other skills in high school that will prove invaluable in life. Master these skills, and you'll rise to the top of the dazzle. You'll be a lead zebra:

- *Time management skills*—do you remember the time you had to study for your math test and had many other important obligations in the same week? You figured out a way to manage your time by not wasting it playing Candy crush or anything else that did not move you closer to achieving your goal.

- *Teamwork skills*—have you ever worked in a group project for class? One of the skills that you learn when working in a group project is teamwork. This is a skill that comes up again and again in college, graduate school, and in working life.

- *Communication skills*—learning how to write a focused and persuasive paragraph or an essay are skills that enable you to become a better communicator. Learning how to speak to another person and a group to present an idea or an argument in a convincing manner will be necessary in your university and professional life as well. Start mastering these communication skills while you're in high school.

- *Leadership skills*—if you have ever led a group or team, you have developed some leadership skills. You may have delegated a task to another student on your team or arbitrated a disagreement between team members. Seize every opportunity you can while in high school to practice being a leader because in your university, professional, and personal life, you'll be called upon to lead many times.

- *Problem-solving skills*—your ability to solve problems will determine whether or not you succeed in the workforce. The "problem solving" I'm referring to in this context means how you tackle tricky situations, assignments, issues, and people by using the resources at hand, drawing from your own experiences, and getting creative. For example, writing a solid research paper requires problem solving. You have to brainstorm the topic. You have to read and learn about it in all its complexities and nuances. Then you have to determine the approach you'll use when presenting the topic in the paper. This kind of problem solving is similar to what you'll be doing in the professional world—when you need to present an idea to a boss or team, or make an argument to management on why you deserve a pay raise or additional vacation time. The many problem-solving situations you are confronted with in high school give you good practice for the many times you'll have to solve problems as an adult. So take advantage of them!

Here's what one of my mentees, Ricardo, shares about his experience with these "other" skills:

*I was never the brightest students in high school or even the hardest working, but I learned two important skills that would help me to succeed immensely: time management and studying. Managing my time didn't come easy for me, but with a little dedication and a lot of discipline, I mastered the skill and became exceedingly more organized and efficient as a result. I began to plan out all of my days in the morning, and they were packed with different activities from being in the marching band, partaking in an after-school college prep program, doing my homework, and even playing video games. Not only was I never late to practice or late on an assignment, I realized I had more time in the day than I previously believed.*

*The second skill is just as important for anyone in school, and it is studying. I learned at a young age that everyone learns differently, and personally I am a visual learner. Also I retain information better if I have to teach it to someone else. If I have pictures, graphs, charts, or anything I can see, I retain the information, but if I have to share the information with another person, I gain an even better understanding of whatever it is I am studying. So, I made it a personal goal to study in groups. These skills helped me to make it to the top of my class and are helping me immensely in college today.*

It will take more than just reading. It will take more than just taking more notes. It's going to take consistent action, implementation, practice, and study of these skills so that you can improve and eventually master them. Be deliberate about seizing opportunities at school and beyond in which you are challenged in those "other" skill areas.

In closing, learning the basics is one thing but mastering the basics is another thing. To succeed like a zebra you will have to master the basics.

Review the benefits and recommendations listed in the chapter as well as a few exercises in the action items section.

## Zebra Action Time

1.  Write down a list of the skills you have learned and are learning in high school.

2.  How does the list relate to what you do on a daily basis? Think of outside of school. Do you ever use any of the skills? Record the amount of times you use the skills in school and out of school.

3.  Play a game with yourself to see how many of the skills you can use a day outside of school. How many did you use today?

## Up Next

In the next chapter we will cover how learning a new language will improve your chances of enjoying even greater success.

# CHAPTER 12

## *Learn a New Language*

---

*One language sets you in a corridor for life.*
*Two languages open every door along the way.*

—Frank Smith

---

*HOLA. ALLO. MARHABAAN.* Hello. There are only three species of zebras in world, and all live in different parts of Africa. Plains zebras live in the treeless grasslands and woodlands of eastern and southern Africa. The Grevy's zebra lives in the arid grasslands of Ethiopia and northern Kenya. The mountain zebra is found in South Africa, Namibia, and Angola. Imagine if any one of these zebras wanted to communicate with zebras of other species, then they would have to learn that other specie's language. Zebras that can speak two or even all three zebra languages are at an obvious advantage. I encourage you too to be a zebra with the most advantages—learn to speak other languages!

Learning to speak a second or third language is something that every high school student needs to do because we're living in a time where those who are bilingual/trilingual thrive. When you speak a second or third language, you have more job and life options. Succeed like a zebra by learning another language.

I can remember in high school taking a French class. It was both good and challenging. Since both my parents come from Haiti, a Creole and French-speaking country, I could see the advantage of learning the language, but at that time, I didn't put in the effort to make it happen. I didn't realize its huge value. Unfortunately, I did not take the class seriously. I just saw it as a grade. As a result, I missed out on a huge opportunity. It's something I regret. I'm telling you this, so you can learn from my mistake. Take advantage of the foreign language classes offered in your high school.

There are many benefits to learning a new language. Yes, all these benefits add to my regret about not taking advantage of my high school French classes, but hopefully you'll learn from my mistake. Here's some of those benefits:

- Learning another language can actually help with reading abilities and linguistic awareness in your native language.

- Studying a second language can raise your SAT and ACT scores.

- Bilingualism improves memory skills and problem-solving abilities.

- Learning a new language raises cultural awareness regarding the cultures that speak the language being learned.

- It can open up your network of friends.

- It can widen your worldview.

- It can increase your vocabulary.

As you can see from the list of benefits above, learning to speak a foreign language goes beyond the classroom. Make a commitment to learning another language while you are in school. Be intentional about it.

# Zebra-Trail-to-Success Beyond the Classroom

The only problem with taking high school language classes is that you are often not taught how to hold conversations well. That's why I recommend using additional resources, so that you can master the language.

Beyond your high school language classes, there are many resources out there to help you master a new language. Some are free and others have a price.

Duolingo is a great resource for learning a foreign language. It is a free website and app that you can access at any time to learn and sharpen your language skills. It incorporates reading, writing, listening, and speaking the new language. Duolingo even offers podcasts. Research shows that Duolingo can be more effective than many paid language learning programs.

Another great online resource is Busuu. The best part of this program is that native speakers correct your writing exercises free-of-charge. However, many of the features require a paid subscription.

The 2017 Nick Zizi Scholarship recipient Saika Senat shared a moving story in her essay submission about her experience learning English as a teenager. Saika was displaced after the 2010 Haiti earthquake destroyed her home. She then had to move to Miami, Florida, to start over. Saika had to get acquainted with a new culture, language, and educational system. In order for her to make friends she needed to learn to speak English. She made it a top goal. She wrote English words and their meanings on index cards and practiced every day. She also challenged herself to only speak English to all of her friends. Eventually she was able to make new English-speaking friends and excell in school. Saika excelled so much that she ended up winning the Nick Zizi Scholarship in 2017. Learning a new language was just one of many skills Saika worked to master on her path to achievement.

Listening to native speakers with songs and podcasts in that foreign language also helps with the learning. I usually listen to talk radio shows and watch the news in French. You can also find audio programs at the library that you can check out, copy, and listen to at your leisure. Usually when learning a foreign language, I repeat out loud what I am listening to to get the proper diction and pronunciation of the words.

The best way to get good at a language is to speak it with a native speaker. Look for a native speaker and start a conversation with them. If you're learning Spanish, you can strike up a conversation with a native speaker at your school in Spanish. The same applies to any language—French, Creole, Chinese, Polish, whatever. At the grocery, on the bus, waiting in line at the movies, strike up a conversation with a native speaker. Then you'll be able to learn and improve fairly quickly. Plus, the person is typically delighted that you are interested in their language and culture.

Don't wait to learn a new language. Take advantage of foreign language classes your high school offers. I know I wish I had! You may not have time later, so start now.

## Zebra Action Time

1.  Write down in your journal why it is important to you to learn a second language.

2.  Write a goal to learn a new language in a year's time in your journal and calendar.

3.  Register for a foreign language class. Which language do you want to learn and why?

4. Download the language applications mentioned above and use them daily.

5. Look for native speakers to converse with on a regular basis. You can find native speakers at school, your neighborhood, or even online. Ideally, it would best to find someone who also wants to learn your language so that you both can help each other in the learning process.

## Up Next

Learning a foreign language goes hand in hand with becoming digitally literate to get the most out of your learning. In the next chapter, we will cover how to become a digitally literate zebra to get the most out of school and life.

# CHAPTER 13

# *Become Digitally Literate*

---

*The ultimate promise of technology is to make us master of a world that we command by the push of a button.*

—Volker Grassmuck

---

THE ZEBRA WITH the smartphone saved her life when the lion tried to attack her. She checked her lion-tracking app and detected the lion's plot. Okay, Zebras don't have smartphones, but they are current with the technology. Top students—or should I say, zebras—are digitally literate. They know how to use technology to be more productive. In order to survive and thrive in college and beyond you must be digitally literate. In other words, you've got to know how to use the technology that's available.

Technological advancements can be daunting. The updates on your smartphone alone are more frequent and sophisticated than they ever were years ago. What about the updates on your computer? Or the updates on the software that you just purchased? So many changes. So many updates.

As I am writing this chapter, I received an email notification concerning the writing software that I purchased three weeks ago. Apparently there is a new fully loaded software update. Wow. What are my options? One, I can just call it quits and say that this is just way too much to take in. Two, I can face the challenge and study, learn, and use the software. I bought the software to improve my productivity and give me more options to facilitate my writing, so I am going to buckle down and learn how to use the software better, even when there are changes from updates. It's important to me that I stay digitally literate, and you'll find it's important for you too—if you want to succeed like a zebra.

Digital literacy is the ability to use digital devices and software. It ranges from seemingly simple things like how to use a mouse, how to scroll, how to cut, copy, and paste a word, a file, or an image, and how to set up an email account, to more complex skills like how to browse and delete your web history and how to set up virus protection to very complex things like how to write code. It also includes the ability to differentiate fact from fiction in online articles and reports, the ability to detect predators (scammers, bullies, and sex predators), and the ability to deal with viruses and scams in general. Digital literacy is necessary for succeeding at school and landing great jobs today.

Learning about the technology that is currently available and knowing what to use will make a tremendous difference in your life. I recall when I was in my last semester in grad school, I was incredibly busy with school itself as well as speaking at various conferences and schools across the nation. During this time, it was extremely difficult to find the time to do the extensive reading assignments. That's when technology came to the rescue. By using the "voice over" feature on my phone, I could listen to my reading assignments while I was working or driving. I was able to keep up with the reading load in my transition time without having to carve out additional time.

Technology can be very helpful, especially in the classroom, because it gives students the opportunity to explore different ways of learning. For example,

Markesner, a junior, and his classmates were having difficulty understanding the various factions and their roles in the American Civil War. Their history teacher allowed them to use their cell phones to search online for additional resources that might be helpful. Markesner found a video entitled "American Civil War in 10 minutes." He watched it and was able to fully understand.

## Resources for Improving Your Digital Literacy

Digitalliteracy.gov is the homepage for the government's digital literacy initiative. It has a large number of links to free articles and videos, which will improve your digital literacy in a range of areas.

Many public libraries also offer computer courses. Your local public library's website can tell you more. Public libraries have computers for their members to use for free as well.

Another great starting point is to create a Gmail account. Gmail is free to use for individuals. Make your email address one you won't mind using for a long time, that is easy to give out, and that looks good on a resume. Using your name with your first and last names separated by a period, hyphen, or underscore is a good way to go. For other Google-related offerings, for instance, to learn how to use Google Drive, Google Docs, Google Photos, etc., you can find free tips and tutorials at apps.google.com.

I am confident that if you take the time to become digitally literate, it will help you in so many ways. For one you will be more productive. Visit digitalliteracy.gov to review additional articles and resources to help you sharpen up your skills. Review what I shared here and you will be on your way to thriving like a zebra.

## Zebra Action Time

1. What do you want to learn and/or improve as it relates to technology?

2. What ways will this learning and improving help you?

3. Make a plan to work on one or two of these areas each week. When do you plan to start and on what area will you focus?

4. What resources will you use to help you sharpen your skills?

## Up Next

Zebras are not only digitally literate; they also get their driver's licenses while in high school. Driving gives you the freedom to get around but comes with great responsibility. We'll investigate this in chapter 14.

# CHAPTER 14

## *Get Your Driver's License*

*A driver's license gives you freedom to drive. Drive responsibly.*

—Nick Zizi

ZEBRAS USUALLY TRAVEL up to 1,800 miles in search of food. This means the zebra has to be vigilant when moving from one place to another. Although a zebra doesn't need a driving license, it still has to prove that it can survive and thrive by moving responsibly, or else a cheetah or lion will cause it to have a serious "wreck."

While it may seem obvious to get your license while you're in high school, there's a great number of students who don't do this. For some, it's due to fear and for others, financial difficulties. I urge you to do all you can to get your driver's license because it will allow you many new opportunities. For example:

- It serves as your official personal ID.

- You'll have more independence with a driver's license, not needing to rely on family, friends, or others to get to school, clubs, games, or work.

- It offers great convenience because you don't have to rely on public transportation.

- Some jobs require a driver's license.

Each state is different, so look up your state's requirements on dmv.org to know all that getting a driver's license entails in your particular state. If your school offers a driver's ed course, take it.

Christy, a teen that I have worked with over the years in our school mentorship program, shared this about her driving experience:

*In 2016 at the age of 16, I got my first official job at Target. I thought it would be super easy to get to and from work, but I was wrong. Having to learn all those Broward County bus routes was a pain. Rain or shine, I had to get to work. One day I remember having to catch the bus in the pouring rain with a tiny little red umbrella—not a great experience. Over the years I finally learned to drive and got my license. Eventually I got my own car. Now I'm more independent, I don't have to rely on my parents anymore not only to take me to work but to take me to school and other places. Knowing how to drive gives me opportunities to get betters job at farther distances because I don't have to think about transit locations to get there. Knowing how to drive gives me confidence. Just like my parents taught me, I can teach someone else.*

## Warning: Avoid These Risks

While I strongly urge you to get a driving license, you need to be aware of some risks so that you can avoid them. In the US the leading cause of death among teenagers, ages 16 to 19, are car crashes and car accidents. Teenagers 16 to 19 are three times more likely to have a fatal car accident than drivers 20 and older. The CDC lists the following as the eight leading causes of teen crashes, so take note of these and do all you can to avoid them.

*One*—number one is driver inexperience. What you can do to reduce this is even after getting a license, continue to practice with an adult. Also, practice with an adult in as many different driving conditions as possible. That means practicing on cloudy and rainy days too. The more exposure you get to various conditions, the more you will improve your skill level in the process.

*Two*—the next cause of accidents is driving with teen passengers. Make sure you follow any state restrictions on passengers for newly licensed drivers. Also, don't have friends as passengers for the first six months. I know that may be hard to do because many of your friends may want to get a ride with you. That would be normal if they're your friends. You too would want them to go with you. However, the first six months, you want to avoid having teen passengers in your car.

*Three*—the next leading cause of death or accidents is nighttime driving. Don't drive after dark for the first six months. It may be challenging to do, especially if you have class or practice during the evening, but it is highly recommended that you do not drive at night. Your vision is limited after dark, and as a new driver you want to make sure all is clear while driving. The time to drive at night is when you can do so with an adult.

*Four*—the other cause of accidents is not using seatbelts. Make sure you wear a seatbelt. Follow the law and wear a seatbelt. Back in the day, there was a seatbelt commercial that I cannot forget. Dummies were used as the driver and passenger in a car that crashed into a wall. Since the dummies did not have their seatbelts on, they were badly damaged. Don't be a dummy; wear a seatbelt at all times.

*Five*—the next cause of accidents is distracted driving. Don't eat, text, talk on a cellphone, or play with the radio while driving. I read a billboard recently that said, "Don't text while you drive so that you can arrive." It can wait. Just drive.

*Six*—the next cause is drowsy driving. Don't drive if you feel tired. In fact, I remember I was so tired one day. I had spent two hours detailing my car, and I was excited as a 19-year-old to have this vehicle. It was nice. It was my first vehicle. I polished it, cleaned it, and took a long time to get it to where I wanted it to be. After picking something up at a friend's and then heading to my cousin's house, I fell asleep behind the wheel. My car swerved and crashed behind my cousin's brand-new car. It was devastating. It was sad, but I learned from that experience: do not drive when you are drowsy.

*Seven*—another cause of accidents is reckless driving. Follow the speed limit. Go even slower if road conditions call for it. Also, leave enough space between the car in front of you and yourself, so if they make a sudden stop, you don't rear-end them. Reckless driving will only cause you to get into a wreck. Drive responsibly.

*Eight*—the final cause of accidents among teens is impaired driving. Don't drive if you've been drinking or taking drugs. Follow the law and avoid mind-altering substances. Keep in mind that some meds cause certain side effects that may affect your judgment, so do not take these kind of prescription drugs before you drive. Consult with your physician to see the best time to take such meds.

In closing, get your driver's license and drive responsibly. A driver's license gives you the privilege to drive. Driving gives you the freedom, the independence you have been longing for. Be a zebra and get your license. Make sure to follow the recommendations shared in this chapter and the action items section as well.

## Zebra Action Time

1.  If you have not yet received your driver's license, when do you plan on getting it?

2.  Register for an approved driver's education course. Each state may have different requirements for this, so check your local DMV to see what's required.

3.  Submit the application. Your parents may have to sign too to give permission for you to drive.

4.  Study. You can take practice exams online and/or go to your local DMV and request a handbook that you can review to better prepare for the exam.

5.  Take the test. You will do well if you take time to prepare.

6.  Drive. Because some states have particular requirements, you may have to log in a certain amount of hours with your learner's permit before you can get your license. So check with your local DMV for more information.

## Up Next

Zebras drive responsibly to the post office to mail out thank-you cards. Your saying thank you to your teacher can make a world of a difference in a demanding and at times underappreciated profession—as you'll learn in the next chapter.

# SECTION 3

## *Build Character*

To stand firm in the midst of chaos, whether being attacked by a lion or migrating through crocodile-infested waters, a zebra must have strong character to survive and thrive. As you migrate through your waters and plains, know that you will need to build your character to succeed like a zebra. In this section we will cover character-building strategies, like leading a team, volunteering, reaching out to someone who may be left out, and more.

# CHAPTER 15

# *Write Thank-You Notes to Your Teachers*

*No one is more cherished in this world than someone who lightens the burden of another. Thank you.*

—Author Unknown

ZEBRAS ARE SOCIAL animals that spend much of their time in a dazzle. They groom one another by licking and biting each other's coats to get rid of dirt and bugs. It's a way of showing their appreciation for one another. Imagine grazing and warding off predators for most of the day—how exhausting it can get. By showing appreciation you can help your teachers cope with the sometimes-overwhelming demands of teaching.

Teachers are some of the most unappreciated professionals. When a person goes into teaching, they're not doing it for money. Normally it's because the person wants to make an impact. What can happen then is that over the years, the hopeful, aspiring teacher gets over-worked. This can lead to burnout and their leaving the profession. However, when students show teachers appreciation, students remind them why they wanted to teach in

Succeed Like a Zebra

the first place. A thank-you note will go a long way to brighten up your teacher's day.

I know this firsthand. I've been on both sides. I was a student, and I'm a teacher as well, so I see the amount of time that it takes to prepare and to go into the classroom and give my best. I know how far-reaching it is when my students show some type of appreciation.

I can count the number of thank-you notes I have received over the years: 20. I still remember the students who went out of their way to show their appreciation: Alex, Elijah, Fredline, and Monica. In fact, I still have some of their cards with me.

I received a small note card at the end of the school year from Monica who shared her appreciation for my teaching that year. She mentioned a time when she was struggling with a leadership concept and how I helped her by explaining it in a way that she could understand. Her thank-you note to me made my day. But she went even farther: she included a gift card, an ice cream gift card with a note that said, "I know you like ice cream, so please accept this as a small token of my appreciation for all you have taught us. Thank you." Wow. She did her research and found something that I liked and added the icing on the cake, if you will.

Whenever I feel the pressure of burnout, I look over these thank-you cards for a boost through the hump. They make such a difference.

Whenever you do something, especially if it's something nice, you want people to appreciate it, right? So whenever you get to a place or time people are not appreciative of what you're doing, how do you feel? You don't feel good. You don't feel like you should continue. You don't feel like you should give your best. By saying thank-you to your teachers, you will motivate them to do their best. Everyone needs that!

There are other great benefits to writing thank-you notes as well. For one, you will stand out from the crowd. Your teachers will remember you. It's a way to also build a relationship, which can be fruitful to you when you apply to college, apply to internships, look for mentors, and apply to jobs. Teachers will be more willing to provide a positive reference letter to you or help you revise and improve your application essays when they have a relationship with you.

Additionally, when you get outside yourself and actually consider another person's good qualities and deeds, which is what you'll have to do when you write the thank-you note, it makes you a more appreciative and grateful person in general. It makes you less self-absorbed. This, in turn, builds your maturity and character.

## The Best Thank-You Notes

Writing a teacher something along the lines of "Thanks for being a great teacher" is nice, but really it's not as thoughtful or personal as it could be. You want your note to really affect your teacher, to really show your sincerity and thoughtfulness, so that will take some personal touches.

Here's how you can write a great thank-you note:

- Don't just write something on notebook paper that you fold up. Purchase a real card that has its own envelope. You can buy a $1 card at the Dollar Store.

- Mention something specific that the teacher has said, done, taught, etc., that you are thankful for in your note. Tell what it was and why you are thankful.

- Write it by hand. Handwritten notes are more personal.

- Don't just leave the card for the teacher on their desk. Hand-deliver the card to your teacher to make it even more personal so that it really builds the relationship between you.

Show appreciation to your teachers by giving thank-you cards. You will make their day and maybe even make their year! Plus you will not only be remembered but can develop a more productive relationship beyond high school with your teachers, which will help you accelerate your success.

## Zebra Action Time

1. Write a list of all of your teachers. Write their names on the list, and then write one thing that you would like to thank them for. Really think this through.

2. Give the letters to your teachers in the last week of school. Hand-deliver the notes too.

3. Bonus: put a small gift card in each card. It could just be a $5 or $10 gift card for coffee or something that you know your teacher will like.

## Up Next

Make your teacher's day by showing appreciation—that's what leaders do. Really though, you can only lead like a zebra by actually leading, which is what we'll address in the next chapter.

# CHAPTER 16

## *Lead a Team, Club, or Class*

---

*Become the kind of leader that people would follow
voluntarily, even if you have no title or position.*

—Brian Tracy

---

PLAINS ZEBRAS AND mountain zebras live in family groups led by a stallion, with several mares and offspring. The dazzle is led by a stallion and has a hierarchy for the mares. When the offspring or foal is of age to start their own family they leave the family group to make their own. Leading like a zebra means to lead your own group.

You can lead. Yes, you. Even if you are an introvert or shy, you can still lead. Perhaps you may already possess great leadership qualities or are in a position of leadership already. This chapter will help you to be a more effective leader. First, let's look at the benefits of developing leadership skills.

Leadership builds self-esteem. Leadership forces you to improve a wide variety of people skills, such as negotiation skills, networking skills, communication skills, and management skills.

You can record your leadership positions on college applications and job resumes, which will make you more impressive and sought-out. Teachers will write you stronger letters of recom-mendation too because they can discuss your amazing leadership qualities.

When I was in high school, I remember doing a social studies group project. Mr. Smith, my teacher, assigned the groups and the leaders. He chose me to be a group leader. At the time I was shy. If I could, I would have crawled into my desk instead of lead a group. Instead of cowering, I stepped up to the challenge. I delegated different tasks and helped set the roles for every team member. The experience taught me how to communicate effectively and delegate. It was an important step on my stairway to becoming an effective leader.

Studies show that people who have leadership roles in high school are more likely to enjoy leadership positions in their careers, for example boss and manager roles. These roles allow you to make more money, as most jobs with supervisory responsibilities pay more.

Anichard, one of my former students, said this about leading:

*While in high school, I was on the step team for two years. I became the department head, meaning the team captain. This role taught me how to be responsible. I was in charge of coming up with the routines, teaching the routine, and making sure everyone was in sync. The progress of the team was on my shoulders. There was no room for error or procrastination. Those lessons that I learned as department head still influence my life even now while I'm in my second year of college.*

## The How

To become a leader of a team, club, or class, first you have to be involved. In a class you are already there, so when opportunities come for group work in projects or even in individual lessons (just a single class period), volunteer to lead your group or the class. For teams and clubs, first you have to join them. Once you are on them, you don't have to be the elected, formal leader to begin leading. You can do small, leadership type things: set up chairs, stay afterwards and help clean up, send out reminder messages, bring water bottles or snacks, etc.

Because leadership is about helping and serving, be sure to vocalize to the class, team, or club organizers that you want to help, that you are looking for ways to contribute. When you serve with that mentality, it will make it easier for you to rise in your leadership position as a servant leader. What you'll find is that over time, you get noticed by your peers and the adults, and this gets you clout and shows your potential. Once you build enough clout and it's time to vote for the leaders, you will be the first choice.

If you worry about your shyness, know many of the leaders you admire have at one time or another dealt with shyness or self-doubt. I, for one, have. As I travel and speak across the nation, I still at times feel like I can't, but I do it anyway. Other leaders who wrestle with shyness include Mark Zuckerberg, Bill Gates, Richard Branson, Will Farrell, and Yara Shahidi. Just like them, you can be shy and still be an effective leader. Don't let shyness or self-doubt prevent you from becoming the best leader that you can be.

To help you land leadership positions and be an effective leader, I recommend checking out books and other leadership-related materials. Here are some books as well as talks on leadership that I highly recommend:

- *The 360-Degree Leader* by John C. Maxwell

- *The Seven Habits of Highly Effective Teens* by Sean Covey

- *How to Win Friends and Influence People* by Dale Carnegie

- TED Talk: How Great Leaders Inspire Action by Simon Sinek

- *21 Irrefutable Laws of Leadership* by John C. Maxwell

Remember: reading a book on leadership will not make you a leader. Theory alone won't cut it. Leading will. Lead and your confidence will come.

# Zebra Action Time

1. First consider your school. What are some clubs, teams, or groups in your school that you would like to get involved with and perhaps eventually lead? How can you apply the "servant leadership" mentality to start your rise to leading the club, team, or group? Think about it and record your thoughts in your journal.

2. You can also look for class leadership opportunities. That is to say, any opportunity to volunteer to do something. You can volunteer to pass out the assignments, write the assignment on the board, or collect papers.

   - Write down what you plan on volunteering to do in your class when the next opportunity presents itself.

   - Another quick example: your teacher may ask for volunteers to set up different groups in class. You can volunteer to lead a group. This will put you in a position where you have to speak, deal with other people, and learn how to be a team player.

3. Keep a record of your progress in your journal. Write about how you are being challenged and what you plan to do to achieve your leadership growth goal. Also, write about your setbacks and victories as

a leader or team member. You will be amazed to see the speed of your growth as a leader. You should also write about what you will improve next time you meet with your team, club, group, or class.

## Up Next

Leaders lead and reach out, which is what chapter 17 discusses. Reach out to someone who may be left out. You never know—you may just save a life.

# CHAPTER 17

## *Reach Out to Someone Who May Be Left Out*

*No one knows for certain how much impact they have on the lives of other people. Oftentimes, we have no clue. Yet we push it just the same.*

— Jay Asher in *Thirteen Reasons Why*

ZEBRAS CARE FOR each other. They are always on the look-out for lions, hyenas, and any other predator. If one is injured they will form a circle around the injured zebra, warding off predators. Zebras care about all the zebras in their dazzle.

Imagine for a moment—you're at school. Your friends are ignoring you. You're walking down the hall, you see your friends, and they act as if they don't see you. How would you feel? How would your week go? How would your month go? Most teens will say they wouldn't feel good at all. No one likes to be excluded. No one wants to be ignored.

The opposite is true. Your smile can brighten up a lonely or hurting student's day. Your welcoming greeting can melt a broken heart. Your concern may just save a life. You never know the magnitude of a little kind gesture on someone's life who may be hurting. And you never know who is hurting.

Over the years, I have had students express their sentiments with me after hearing my presentations. The ones that hit me the hardest were the teens on the brink of giving up on life. They told me things like this:

- *I lost my mother to cancer, I don't want to continue anymore. She was the reason I worked so hard in school. You asked me what my mother would want. She'd want me to work hard, so I will continue to work hard for her legacy. Thank you.*

- *I usually cut myself when I feel depressed. What you shared today about loving ourselves really resonated with me. I will seek professional help and replace cutting with something like drawing or exercising. Thank you so much.*

- *Although I didn't seem to show much interest during your presentation, I was absorbing it all. It came right in time. You shared your story about the time you were struggling in school and how you turned yourself around. Prior to hearing you I wanted to give up because I have tried to bring my grades up while trying to help my parents pay the bills. It seemed nearly impossible, but I will keep pushing like a zebra to make it work.*

And just by listening to my message, they became inspired, motivated, and hopeful. You can have the same impact too.

When I was a student in summer school, there was a student who would sit in the front row of my math class. His name was Jeremiah, and he was picked on every day, simply because he was obviously poor. He seemed to ignore the cruel comments that other students made about his tattered clothes and worn-out shoes. Although I did not join in the name-calling, I chuckled with everybody else.

He remained silent. No one knew what was on his mind because he kept quiet. I could tell that he was troubled but did not want to speak up. There could be many reasons why he did not speak. He may have lost his parents or had something horrific happen in his life. I didn't know.

If I could go back, I would have reached out to him. First, I would have asked my classmates to stop the name-calling. Second, I would have conversed with him to get to know him better. I'd ask: how are you? How do you like the class? Do you like sports? If yes, what's your favorite team? The point here is to show interest and find something that we would have in common to build from there. Third, I would donate clothing and shoes to him. Lastly, I would try my best to be a friendly face interested in his success at the school daily. If I could go back in time, I'd do all those things with no second thought.

This chapter's message is so important. I urge you to do it, not just once but often. Reach out to someone who may be left out. Sometimes it is apparent; you can see the person sitting by themselves. Or they may be the student you saw the other day getting picked on. Reach out to that person.

## Zebra-Trail-to-Success for Reaching Out

There are many ways that you can do it. First, you look for them; you can see them sitting at the cafeteria table by themselves. Go and sit next to them or invite them to sit at your table with your friends. Make a compliment. Look for something that you like about them. Perhaps it's their hairstyle or sneakers. You can make a sincere compliment to let the person know that you appreciate them.

You can also buy lunch for that person. You can look for what you share in common. Perhaps it's sports, a certain actor, a movie, a song. Build the relationship on common ground. Let the person know that you're there for them.

Know that you may not be welcomed. Your kind gestures may be taken as an insult—or as you showing them pity. That's okay. When people are hurting, they may have been hurt so much that it seems that they don't appreciate any kindness. Here's a word to the wise: don't be weary in well-doing. Continue to reach out. Love trumps hate and heals hurt.

Nancy, a junior, confided that she noticed a student who was always alone. One day Nancy approached the girl and asked why she was always alone. The student expressed that she wanted to be alone. Nancy continued asking questions to dig deeper. She discovered that the student felt left out because of the cruel comments others had made throughout the year, for example, calling her a weirdo. Nancy told this girl that she at one time experienced similar rejection, but she dealt with it by seeing herself as someone valuable. The girl's facial expression revealed her relief and joy to know that she was not alone.

Treat them—and everyone—the way you would like to be treated. That is the Golden Rule. Consider how you would like people to treat you if you were hurting or dealing with a situation where your friends have excluded you. Do that for the students who are the loners or maybe the oddballs. You may just save a life.

Show that you care by reaching out. Even just a smile. A greeting. Your concern may just save a life. Reach out.

## Zebra Action Time

1. Think of all the people that may feel left out. Write a list of their names if you know them; if not, write a short description of the person so that you can remember to identify who they are.

2. Are there any other people who are not on your list that may be friends that you have not seen in a while? If yes, write their names and a date when you plan to contact them to see how they are doing.

3. Plan a time when you are going to reach out to these people. If you don't plan it, it may never happen. Will you reach out today? If not, when? How often?

4. Make reaching out something that you do on a regular basis. Those who may be hurting or excluded will appreciate the gesture and feel that you care. How do you plan to show that you care?

5. If there is a life-threatening situation (suicidal thoughts included) that the person is dealing with, let the appropriate authorities know, preferably a teacher, counselor, or principal. You can save someone's life by reaching out. Start today.

## Up Next

Reaching out can save a life just as volunteering can help save a life or make people's lives better. Let's look at volunteering more closely in the next chapter.

# CHAPTER 18

## *Volunteer*

---

*Everybody can be great. Because anybody can serve.*
*You don't have to have a college degree to serve.*
*You don't have to make your subject and your verb*
*agree to serve . . . You don't have to know the second*
*theory of thermodynamics in physics to serve. You only*
*need a heart full of grace. A soul generated by love.*

—Martin Luther King, Jr.

---

ZEBRAS GROOM EACH other in the wild. They have a heart of service. A zebra will help other zebras remove ticks and debris, so that their zebra buddies are clean, healthy, and happy. When one zebra helps another zebra stay clean and healthy, overall it helps the whole dazzle. Service to one person in need betters the community as a whole—it's true for humans too!

It's been said that service is the rent that we pay for the space that we occupy here on Earth. Your life and world will never be the same again when you make the deliberate effort to volunteer on a regular basis. You can volunteer through service groups at your school, through non-school affiliated organizations, like soup kitchens and shelters, and churches too often do community service. The point is to help others who are in need.

There are many benefits to volunteering. First and foremost, the work you are doing betters someone or something else. Another person, place, animal, or plant benefits simply because you give your time, energy, and mind to it. That's a big deal. For example, if you decide to walk dogs at an animal shelter, those dogs and the people who run the shelter are enjoying better conditions because of you. If you spend a day picking up trash along the side of the road, that environment, drivers, and home-dwellers all benefit because you've removed the visual blight and polluting debris. If you volunteer at a soup kitchen, dishing out food to people who cannot afford food themselves, they benefit from your volunteering.

But really, you—the volunteer—will enjoy a ton of benefits too. Volunteering helps you feel better about yourself. Studies show that volunteering increases happiness. It adds meaning to your life. If you do a social volunteering activity—where you are working with other volunteers or recipients, then you can enjoy social benefits, such as making friends and improving your social skills. Volunteering improves mental and physical health. You can get community service hours too.

Jonas, a sophomore, volunteered at Scott Lake Elementary School, assisting with cleaning, organizing classrooms, and even teaching a class. He said that he had a lot of fun and felt happy working with the teachers and students. When asked if he would do it again, Jonas told me, "Of course, it's the best feeling in the world to serve others."

There is another great benefit as well: you can gain career experience and learn job skills while helping. The type of volunteering you are doing will determine the type of skills you learn. Let's say you volunteer to make phone calls for a non-profit seeking more donors, then you will learn a ton about persuading and selling the idea of what the organization stands for.

As a result, you will become a better communicator and salesperson. You see, volunteering is a win-win.

You win, and the organization wins. The people who are being served also win. You are not losing anything when you help. You just want to be strategic with your service so that you can make a more significant impact in others' lives and yours too.

As a sophomore, Marsha volunteered to help out in any way she could at school, church, and around the community. Whether it was to help tutor elementary students or take out the trash, Marsha did it. Her heart of service landed her her first job after high school as the school's aftercare director.

There are volunteer positions for all types of interests. If you're interested in helping kids, there are different options for that. If you want to help with feeding the poor, there are many opportunities there as well. If you're interested in taking care of abandoned animals, there are volunteer positions for that.

You can volunteer at a hospital. Some hospitals provide free meals and healthcare, flu shots, annual check-ups, etc., for their volunteers, and that's a great added incentive to volunteer at a hospital. You can also volunteer at homeless shelters. That would put you in contact with members of a group you may have had little contact with. Be aware that many homeless shelters will not accept volunteers under the age of 18.

Another way that you can volunteer is doing Thanksgiving Day volunteering. You can give out sandwiches on Thanksgiving. Serve at a shelter to feed the homeless or the hungry on this day. You can help give out turkeys or canned foods on this day too.

Another option for service work is to help a charity raise money. For instance, you could sell candy bars door-to-door, solicit restaurants to offer "donate a dollar" days, or organize a community or school walk or run to raise money for a charity. In addition to raising money, collecting donations, such as clothing, toiletries, and canned foods, is also appreciated by charities. Fundraising is a great type of service work because it definitely benefits the organization and at the same time allows you to practice your persuasion skills, which are important to doing good interviews and to working in groups.

You can go to the website pointsoflight.org for more information on volunteering opportunities near you. It is a nonprofit that promotes volunteering and helps connect volunteers to organizations needing help.

You don't have to wait until you are older or out of school to do volunteer work. Your service will mean the world to those in need. The best time to start is right now. Follow the suggestions listed in the chapter and complete the action items to start serving like a zebra.

## Zebra Action Time

1. Write down your areas of interest in your journal. Your area of interest is something that you already have a passion for, something that you currently enjoy doing. For example, you may want to be a nurse. That would be an interest in the medical field, in helping others who are incapacitated, whether through sickness or other ailments. You could look for medically-related volunteer opportunities.

2. Think of possible ways you can volunteer in your area of interest. I would strongly urge you to look for volunteer opportunities related to one of your interests. However, don't limit your service. Serve wherever you can.

3. Visit pointsoflight.org to search for volunteer opportunities in your area. Sign up for the ones that are apropos to what you want to do.

4. How often are you willing to volunteer? Will it be weekly, monthly, or quarterly? Keep in mind that regular volunteering is best. You may have less time during the month of your midterms, so plan accordingly.

## Up Next

In the next chapter we will cover how trying out for a sports team can develop your leadership and teamwork skills.

# CHAPTER 19

## *Try Out for the Team*

*Sports teaches you character, it teaches you to play by the rules, it teaches you to know what it feels like to win and lose-it teaches you about life.*

—Billie Jean King

ZEBRAS ARE TEAM players. They run together in a dazzle, not just to survive but to thrive. A lion in attack mode will try to single out a zebra to kill. However, since lions are color blind, when zebras team up, the resulting mass of black and white stripes makes it hard for the lion to single out a zebra. This only works when zebras are moving as a team. You too can thrive in school and life by playing team sports.

I recall many years ago when I played JV football for North Miami Senior High School. It was a sunny Wednesday afternoon after school. We were in a very close game against American Senior High School. I was the first string linebacker, and on the last play as I blitzed, the quarterback juked left, and I went flying right. He sprinted into the end zone. We lost the game. While my coach was upset because we'd lost such a close game, his main message to us was how to handle the loss and to learn from it.

I took this close loss personally and made a commitment to work harder. I pushed myself in every area, from the drills to the weight room. I was determined to get better. I learned too that it took a team to win. I could not do it alone. So I looked for ways to push my teammates in every area to practice harder and work out harder.

I learned leadership and teamwork and so much more playing football—learning that I still benefit from today. Playing a team sport like football taught me to work with others for a common goal. Today as I lead my business organizations and a nonprofit, I utilize what I have learned to play as a team to achieve greater goals.

You learn teamwork when you play sports. Sports will teach you that it is not a one-man or one-woman show. To win you will need to play along with others and do it well. Teamwork learned through sports can transcend into other areas or careers.

Exercise gives lots of health benefits, including reducing stress and increasing your energy levels and happiness. Being on a team is great motivation to exercise. Skipping out on a team practice is harder than skipping a gym session you scheduled for yourself.

My message to you: try out for a sports team, even if you don't consider yourself the athletic type. If sports tryouts or sports in general are new, know that trying new things has a large number of benefits, including increased self-esteem and social engagement. Tryouts are good practice for doing things in front of a crowd or judges. Michael Jordan, arguably the greatest basketball player ever, was cut from his high school basketball team. He's the one that the Lebrons, Kobes, and others looked up too. If Jordan tried out, so should you.

When he was a freshman, Samuel played on his school's baseball team. He said that the team concept has since helped him tremendously in his professional life as a correctional officer. In his job where he is dealing with some of the most dangerous people in the United States, the acronym TEAM—together everyone achieves more—could not be truer. As a correctional officer, it would be impossible to operate or get through even a single day where everyone is safe without communication, discipline, and having trust in his colleagues around him. Samuel explained, "I still must do my part because a team is only as strong as its weakest link, so taking the time to study and hone my skills to best do the job is imperative to the success of the team. A win in sports depends on the entire team, and it's no different in my career. Without a good team around me, failure is imminent."

Try out for a team at your school. It doesn't have to be the most popular sport but one you like, for example golf, ultimate frisbee, or soccer. You don't even have to play for the whole season. Try out for the team so that you can succeed like a zebra.

## Zebra Action Time

1. Make a list of the sports you want to try out for.

2. Check your school's website or athletic department to see which sports programs your school offers. Write down the top three sports your school offers.

3. Contact the coach or director to see when you can try out. What is the coach's name and when do you plan to contact them?

4. Prepare. Get in shape. Exercise. How do you plan to get in shape for the sport you want to try out for? Consider asking the coach for some advice on this.

5.  Practice the basics of the sport. For example, in basketball, you need to know how to dribble, shoot, defend, and rebound. What are the basics of the sport?

6.  Try out. Give it your best shot. Go in with the mindset that you will make the team. How did it go? How do you feel?

## Up Next

In the next chapter we will cover the reason why and how zebras apologize to thrive in their relationships in school and life.

# CHAPTER 20

## *Apologize and Admit Wrongdoing*

*An apology is the super glue of life.*
*It can repair just about anything.*

—Lynn Johnston

PLAINS ZEBRAS ARE highly social and their family group can stay together from a few months to years. A zebra family group can consist of one stallion, several mares, and their offspring. In almost any relationship or group conflicts occur. Plains zebras are able to keep their family groups together because of this one strategy: admitting wrongdoing and apologizing.

Many relationships fall apart when someone does not acknowledge their wrongdoing and continues to strain the relationship until it falls apart. Lesly and Mike were good friends who would go to the library almost on a daily basis together to study and do homework. Someone hacked Mike's account and tagged all his friends on social media to perverted images and videos. Lesly simply assumed what he was seeing was true; he never even considered it could be a hack. So, he made a sarcastic remark about it to

Mike. Also he made obscene comments about Mike's friends and to him directly, calling Mike a "pervert." Mike was hurt, sad, and shocked at how Lesly was treating him. Lesly never apologized and acted as if nothing was wrong. That placed a strain on their relationship until one day Mike exploded at Lesly. In the end apologies were needed to repair the relationship.

There are great benefits to apologizing. Research shows that people who admit their wrongdoing are happier than those who do not. Secondly, your relationships will be stronger when you are able to deal with the problem at hand. Thirdly, you'll experience less conflict. Reduced conflict means less stress. Fourthly, it may lead to the path of forgiveness. The person may be willing to forgive you then.

Chrisla recounts her experience in her senior year with her parents:

*Everyone knows that for senior year class pictures you want to look your best, from your wardrobe to your hair. When it was time for my senior pictures, I decided to get my hair colored and cut. Both of my parents were upset with me for doing this, but my father was disappointed the most. During a conversation, I raised my voice at my father. He ended up getting even more upset.*

*When I took a few minutes to think about what I'd done, I felt hurt and ashamed for raising my voice at my parents. I decided to return to my father and apologize not only for my wrongdoing but for raising my voice at him as well. Apologizing strengthened our relationship, and I've learned to say, "I'm sorry," when I am wrong. In the end I removed the dye, and my senior picture came out great. My parents were pleased in the end.*

Admitting your wrongdoing may be hard to do. One of the reasons is because you are admitting guilt. Keep this in mind that you are not responsible for the other person's part, only your part. That means you are responsible for your actions. Another reason apologies can be difficult is they entail adding attention to a problem that you wish would just go away.

However, it is dangerous to act as if there is no elephant in the room. If there is one, deal with it before it gets worse.

There was a student, whom I will call Tommy, who was talking loudly while the substitute teacher was presenting the lesson. Tommy felt that he could act in a disorderly way since his teacher wasn't there. When I heard news about this, I spoke with Tommy outside of the classroom. I explained to him that talking loudly during a lesson is wrong and rude. I told him to apologize to the sub, but Tommy said no. He felt like if he did that, he would be admitting guilt.

What this told me is that Tommy was not mature enough to take responsibility for his actions. Tommy had a long way to go if he wanted to succeed like a zebra.

An apology comes often when someone knows that they have hurt someone. It can come later when the person senses that someone may not show hurt but is offended by what was said or done.

## How to Apologize

- Know the timing—apologize when you know you have hurt someone or when you are made of aware of it.

- Take ownership—what you said or did that may have hurt a person. Don't own their part, but do own yours.

- Express your regret—show that you are sorry for what you did. It has to be sincere. Don't just say, "I'm sorry." Show it. It needs to come from the heart.

- Tend to the hurt—take care of the wound by sincerely apologizing and correcting your actions.

- Forgiveness—be open to it. Keep in mind that the preceding steps must happen first.

- Set boundaries and stay within them—when a line is crossed in a relationship with your parents, teachers, or anyone, for that matter, there is a dent in it. The more you cross the line by saying whatever pops in your mind to the other person without first thinking, the greater the strain will be. Establish the lines and the relationship will not have to endure the same mistake again.

What if the person you are apologizing to doesn't accept your apology? Know that may happen. Some people are more sensitive than others. That is to say that some can get hurt more than others. Let's say you go to Jimmy and apologize for sharing a secret that he only shared with you. He may be very hurt. If you get to that point, let it go. If you hold on to the fact that he has not accepted your apology, you are now a prisoner. Let it go so that you can grow.

I remember a time when I came back home from work and greeted my wife with excitement, but she gave me the cold shoulder as her welcome. I knew something was wrong but was not sure what it was. I had left early that morning to work on crafting a speech for an upcoming event. I later realized I'd been so focused on my speech that the chores I was supposed to do totally slipped my mind. I then rushed to her and apologized. She, in turn, did not believe it because I had done that same thing before. So now, instead of saying, "I'm sorry," I not only apologize, but I do the thing that I was supposed to do. By supporting my apology with action, I add a lot of sincerity to it. If possible, you should do the same.

There is one more thing you need to do: make sure you work on not repeating the mistake.

In closing, apologizing may be hard to do, but it is worth it. Apologizing may seem like a weakness, but it is a strength. As you may have concluded, it takes a strong person to apologize for a wrongdoing. Save your relationships by admitting when you are wrong and doing the necessary to stay within the boundaries.

## Zebra Action Time

1.  Is apologizing hard for you? If yes, why? If no, why?

2.  What are the benefits of apologizing?

3.  Are there any relationships that you need to make amends with?

4.  Are there people who may have been hurt by what you said or did that you don't feel was a big deal? Write their names and the incident. Plan to meet or call these people to better understand their pain and apologize. If need be, explain that you did not intend to hurt them.

5.  What are some of the changes you will make?

## Up Next

In the next chapter will cover a virtue that every zebra needs to have to thrive in school and life—courage.

# CHAPTER 21

## *Be Courageous:*
## *Do The Right Thing*

*Have the courage to say no. Have the courage to
face the truth. Do the right thing because it is right.
These are the magic keys to living your life with integrity.*

—W. Clement Stone

ZEBRAS DEFEND AND form a circle around a zebra that is under attack to ward off the predator. This takes courage, but zebras know it's the right thing to do. You should be a zebra. Be courageous, do the right thing. It can be quite challenging to do what's right when everyone around you seems to be doing what's wrong, but it's the best thing to do.

I remember reading about a 17-year-old high school football player who worked in the parking lot at a supermarket. He would return shopping carts from the outside to the inside, and he would help customers unload groceries from their carts into their cars. One day he found a wallet that had $1,500 in it. Guess what happened next? He returned the wallet to the store manager who then contacted its owner. This was just one of many items that he found and returned. His coach often told his players, "Don't go astray, but always do right. You can always do right." Apparently, this young man was listening. I urge you to muster the courage to do what is right too.

## How to Do Right When Under Pressure

You can always do right. Be courageous, face the crowd, face your friends, and let them know what you want to do. If they're pressuring you to do something that you don't want to do, there are several things you can do to handle it.

*One*—you can simply say no. Saying no actually empowers you. It puts you in the position of a leader and not a follower. It can be very difficult to do, but it is the most effective. Say no to drugs and to anything that goes against your values.

*Two*—you can argue to your friends that you'll have to deal with consequences from your parents that just aren't worth it to you. You'll lose your phone, your car, your privileges, etc. Your friends should understand this and back off the pressure.

*Three*—mentally take a step back and remember what you really want to achieve in your life. Look at your life in the big picture. With that perspective in mind, evaluate whether doing what your friends are telling you to do makes sense. If it's not the best thing to do, step away from it, and don't do it. Focus on doing the right thing.

*Four*—surround yourself with the right type of people who will encourage you to do good. If you notice that your current friends are not the right influence for you, look for new friends. The so-called "friends" who pressure you to do wrong are not really your friends. Go to where the positive, hard-working students gather to meet the right type of people.

As a sophomore Michelle dealt with negative peer pressure. She and her two friends went to the mall to purchase items for a group project. After she and her friend purchased their items, the other friend did not want to buy anything there, so they left to go to Walmart. On their way out the friend opened her bag to show them what she'd stolen. She encouraged Michelle and the other friend to steal too. They returned to the store, and her friend popped open an Apple headphone box and stuffed the headphones into her pocket. The other friend did the same thing. All three of them were caught, but Michelle was released because she did not steal anything. All through the entire experience, she'd been telling her friends not to steal. In this situation Michelle chose to do the right thing and even tried to get her friends to do the right thing too, but it didn't work. At least, Michelle maintained her courage and didn't cave in. That takes character. That's what a zebra does.

Doing the right thing is a choice. You have to be courageous like a zebra and choose to do the right thing, even in the face of strong predators. Choose to do the right thing.

## Zebra Action Time

1. Was there ever a time when you did something you regretted? What was it? Why did you do it? If you had a chance to do it over, what would you do differently? Reflect on this in your journal.

2. Next, in your journal, write a reflection about doing the right thing when it didn't seem to be popular.

3. If you're being pressured to do something by your friends that is inappropriate or that will get you into trouble, you can always ask for help. You can speak to your parents, guardians, teachers, or counselors about it, and they will help you navigate the situation.

4. Get an accountability partner who will help keep you on-track. Accountability is a powerful influence when you know that there are people who will be checking on you on a regular basis to make sure you're following through on what you said you would do. This helps you do the right thing.

5. Practice saying no. Say no when it goes against what you stand for. Say no when it breaks the rules. You will notice that you feel empowered when you do so.

## Up Next

Being courageous also means stepping out to beautify your community, as explored in the coming chapter!

# CHAPTER 22

# *Join a Beautification Project in Your Community*

I *alone cannot change the world, but I can cast a stone across the waters to create many ripples.*

—Mother Teresa

A ZEBRA'S HABITAT is key to its survival. Depending on the type of species, some zebras live in green plains others live in the mountains. No matter the habitat, if it is dirty or polluted, it makes survival challenging for them. A dirty habitat also decreases their levels of motivation and happiness. This is also true for us in our habitats.

Your community is your habitat. By doing your personal best to keep your neighborhood clean and by joining local beautification groups, you ensure that everyone in your community lives better, more happily, and more safely.

Currently, my wife and I are searching for a new home for our growing family. Our top priority in our home search is a clean and elegant community. There was one home in pristine condition with fabulous features. However, its neighborhood was not well kept. Dead tree limbs hung from trees, and many yards featured overgrown lawns. So, we didn't make an offer on the house. A dirty or ugly community will keep people and opportunities away. Home values drop. These kinds of conditions often welcome vandalism and crime to neighborhoods too.

Happily, the reverse is true: when a community is well maintained, it is more likely to attract businesses, considerate and family-minded residents, and opportunities for further growth. People are happier and friendlier when they live in a clean neighborhood. The more beautiful the neighborhood, the better the mood. Also, the better the people behave. Research shows people are more attached to their communities when those communities are clean and well maintained.

If you already live in a well-maintained, clean community, fabulous. Do all you can do to keep it that way. If your community's appearance is lacking, seize that opportunity to make a difference, to be the change needed. For example, next time you see trash on the ground, whether a candy wrapper, empty bottle, or a plastic bag, even though you didn't drop it there, decide to take on that responsibility and pick it up.

Littering is like dropping trash in your living room or bedroom. Don't ever think that littering is okay. It is not okay. Dumping trash in the street is not cool. Earlier today, as I was driving in a beautiful neighborhood, the driver in front me dropped a bubble gum wrapper out the car window and into the middle of the street. Litterbugs will get swatted. Keep your community clean.

Michael was tired of seeing trash in his neighborhood. He decided to spend one to two hours on Saturdays to keep his streets clean. He would pick up cans, bottles, paper, and anything else that he had the energy and means to collect. His neighbors appreciated his efforts and supported him by keeping their properties clean as well.

In addition to acting on your own, you can form or even join a group that works on beautifying the neighborhood on a regular basis. Some group project ideas include painting fences, planting pretty flowers, picking up trash, and helping those in need to make small house or yard repairs.

To find out more about the many other activities for beautifying your neighborhood, check with your city. If there are ongoing beautification projects in your community, your city hall will know about them. If you want to start your own, talk to the city before you start to make sure you're following the rules.

The website useful-community-development.org has useful advice on what beautification projects have the most significant impact and how to do them well from professional city planners.

In 2015 over 200 students volunteered to clean and beautify Flint, Michigan. They removed debris, planted flowers, boarded up abandoned homes, and much more. They made a difference by volunteering with the beautification project. You too can make a difference by joining your community's beautification project—or by starting such a project if your community doesn't yet have one. Your help will make your surroundings safer, happier, and nicer. Join today. Make a difference.

## Zebra Action Time

1. Visit your city hall's website or office to inquire about any beautification projects currently going on. Find out what the projects are and how you can apply.

2. If your city does not have a beautification project, find out how you can start one. What are the requirements for starting one?

3. Plan to contribute today. You don't need to be in a project or group to keep your neighborhood clean. If you see litter on the street, clean it up. You can start by just picking up any cans on your walk back from school. The point here is not to be the trash collector; the point is to do what you can. Starting today.

4. As mentioned, visit useful-community-development.org for advice from professional city planners on which beautification projects have the most significant impact and how to do them well. After investigating this site, what are the recom-mendations you will implement and when do you plan on doing it?

## Up Next

Making a difference by beautifying your habitat is what zebras appreciate. Another way to make a difference is to travel. Travelling like a zebra affords you experience and knowledge necessary to succeed at a higher level.

# CHAPTER 23

## *Travel*

---

*The world is a book and those who
do not travel read only one page.*

—Augustine of Hippo

---

ZEBRAS ARE ALWAYS on the move, seeking better places to graze. Moving about helps the zebra find better nourishment, which enables them to thrive. Moving about or traveling will have the same positive effect on you.

A good friend and mentor of mine, Johnson Napoleon, who is also a very successful entrepreneur shared with me the value of traveling. He and his family travel around the world. He said that when you travel you immerse yourself in another culture, which will increase your creativity. He has used many of the ideas he picked up from traveling in his business, which has enabled him to boost his sales. For example, he saw a billboard in China for a news station that caught his eye. He took a photo of the billboard and sent it to his graphic designer, who then applied its color scheme and font to create a new billboard for one of Johnson's businesses. With a newly designed billboard using some of the elements from what he saw in China, he received three times the amount of calls as before.

Another reason why you should travel is that it encourages you to become a more compassionate person. My parents are from Haiti. When I visited Haiti, it was a life-altering experience. I remember waiting for an outdoor church conference to start when a young man approached me. He needed money for transportation for school. He had not been able to find a job in over a year and was trying to make ends meet while furthering his education. When I gave him $20, his eyes widened in shock. He gave me a bear hug and told me that God would bless me. Also he told me that the amount I gave him would last him for the rest of month. What was striking is that despite all of his troubles, this man was determined to further his education. I came back home from my travels in Haiti with a greater sense of compassion for others and appreciation for what I have.

Traveling also expands your education. Just think for a moment about a place you have studied in your history class. The pictures and videos are helpful to understanding the location. However, visiting the actual destination and seeing where the events took place adds a whole other level to your learning that cements the information in your mind. It's one thing to read about a place and another to be there.

Georgiana, a junior, told me this about traveling:

*I had the privilege of traveling to the country of Samoa located in the South Pacific—a long way from my home! I lived there for four months for an internship with the United Nations and had the opportunity to really immerse myself in the local culture. I learned so much about the history of the South Pacific, ate different kinds of food, and explored the entire island. Traveling allowed me to understand that there's always something new to learn every day. Learning never stops! The more you are open to learning about other people and places, the more well-rounded you become.*

# Start Small and Build

You don't have to travel to Europe, Africa, or South America, spending lots of money on plane tickets and hotels, to enjoy the benefits of travel. Even something as simple as

getting dinner in a different part of town can expose you to a different set of people and architecture that you aren't used to. Another option is to eat at a restaurant that serves food from an ethnic group whose food you've never eaten before. Have you ever eaten Syrian food? Jamaican food? Ecuadorean food? Russian food? Ethiopian food?

If you do want to travel to another part of the country or the world, after you get your parents' permission, you can pursue volunteer opportunities as a way to keep the costs down or to find travel that is free. You can go to gooverseas.com for a list of international volunteer opportunities that high school students can participate in for free.

Mission trips will allow you to go to a different part of the world and volunteer there during school breaks. Most companies that run travel-learning trips for high school students have scholarship programs that will help you to pay your way while you're there.

Michael went on his first mission trip to South Africa in the summer with his youth group. It was life-altering for him. He never saw kids in such dire need. There was one kid who only wore shorts and had no shirt or shoes who asked Michael for money. He felt so moved that he gave him all the change he had in his pockets. Michael never forgot the feeling he had knowing that he could make a difference.

Traveling will change your worldview. Your life will never be the same again. Your creative juices will be firing away when you see what others like you are doing with what they have. Travel like a zebra.

## Zebra Action Time

1.  Write a list of places you would like to visit while you are in high school. Remember to include new places in your region that you could explore in a single day as well as other states in the US and other countries.

2.  Post the list where you can see it every day.

3.  Search for pictures representing the different destinations you would like to travel to and paste them to your travel list.

4.  Search for travel opportunities for high schoolers. You can review the list of suggestions from gooverseas.com.

5.  Fill out and submit the application before the deadline.

## Up Next

Traveling and following a budget go hand-in-hand. One of the most important skills you will learn is how to make and follow a budget. Let's learn about ASAP in the next chapter!

# SECTION 4

## *Prepare for the Future*

Zebras are ready to win by preparing for the future. In this section, we cover strategies that will help you get ready for your bright future. You will learn how to create a resume, make and follow a budget, master the interview, get a job, and much more.

# CHAPTER 24

## *Make and Follow a Budget*

---

*Manage your spending by creating and sticking to a budget.*

—Alexa Von Tobel

---

A ZEBRA STAYS within its means. If it overextends itself, eating too much grass or resting too much, it runs the risk of being an easy prey. Zebras follow a budget in the sense of strategically thinking things through—so can you. As a teenager, you may have a part-time job or receive an allowance. Following a budget will help you to stay within your means while saving and investing your hard-earned money.

Let me begin by saying that this will not be a comprehensive chapter on money. There is so much to cover on how to make, save, invest, and spend money that we will not have the time to cover every detail. However, I want to pique your interest and help you start your journey to financial mastery.

Would you like to save money? Of course you would. Would you like to multiply the money that you saved? I'm sure you would. Making and following a budget will help you in that regard and much more.

You want to make and follow a budget so that you can stay within your means. When you exceed your means, that's the time when you become stressed. That's the time when you are unable to sleep at night. A budget allows you to know exactly how much money you have at any given time. You'll know your bank account's balance, so you won't get overdrawn, which means you spent more money than you have in your account. When this happens, the bank charges you a hefty penalty fee called an "overdraft fee." Making and following a budget allows you to avoid overdraft fees.

Martine learned about making and following a budget in her junior year. She used to find herself out of cash for most of the time during the week. When she started to make and follow a budget, her money lasted the whole week. She never ran out. She said following a budget helped her keep track of her money. She now thinks twice before making a purchase.

The way a budget works is that you record how much money you have and how much money you are spending—right down to the penny. Every time you buy something, you must subtract that amount to get your new total. You can do this using an app or in a notebook. Every time you spend money, you update your budget. This helps you in a few ways. First of all, you always know how much total money you have, your balance. When you know this, you can be sure never to overspend. Also, you can review each week what it is you are spending your money on. You may notice certain trends—for example—spending money on pricey coffee drinks—and with this realization, you might decide to make other choices so that you can have more money for other things.

Maintaining a budget and reviewing it helps you to be conscious of how you're spending your money. As a result of being more conscious, you will spend more wisely.

It is recommended that you set a budget for every week. You may have different spending/expense limits for different weeks. For example, for week one, your spending limit may be $50; week two, it may be $30. The point is that it varies depending on your allowance and/or job income. When you know your limit, you are more likely to stay within the limit (and avoid penalties for going over it), and you're more likely to spend that limited amount of money wisely so that your money lasts the whole week— rather than you accidentally spending it all the first day of the week!

There are several websites that share more tips on how to make and follow a budget. I recommend the following:

- The site mymoney.gov is the government's financial literacy site. Check it out.

- On moneyandstuff.info you'll find a financial glossary and detailed budget worksheet.

- Onteensguidetomoney.com you'll find very detailed and technical information.

- On benzinga.com there are 10 personal finance apps for teens and young adults.

You should be familiar with the following financial terms:

- *budget*—a spending plan or a record of projected and actual income and expenses over a period

- *credit*—an agreement to provide goods, services, or money in exchange for future payments with interest by a specific date or according to a specific schedule. The use of someone else's money for a fee

- *debt*—something owed, usually measured in dollars

- *saving*—the process of setting income aside for future spending. Saving provides ready cash for emergencies, short-term goals, and funds for investing

- *savings account*—a financial institution deposit account that pays interest and allows withdrawals.

- *interest rate*—how much interest is paid by borrowers for the money that they borrow. It is usually a percentage of the sum borrowed.

Making and following a budget is a very important part of creating the future that you want. You want to start early with this. Make and follow a budget. You can make and follow a budget today and see where you get to by the end of the week.

## Zebra Action Time

1. Download the budget worksheet from moneyandstuff.info and start using it.

2. Plan your week accordingly.

3. Make sure to log in every expense down to the penny daily by using the MINT app or any of the tracking apps at benzinga.com. Another option is to log in your expenses in a notebook.

4. If you ever go over your budget, review the expenses and either increase your limit or remove an item to stay within the budget.

5. Get smarter about your money by reading, researching, and learning all that you can about money. Sign up for classes, watch videos, and ask mentors about money. Save, earn, invest, and continue to learn.

## Up Next

After you have worked out your budget, create your resume to put yourself in the best position to get the job you deserve. Chapter 25 will teach you how to do that!

# CHAPTER 25

## *Create Your Resume*

---

*The best way to predict the future is to create it.*

—Abraham Lincoln

---

A ZEBRA'S RESUME will show that it is best fit for the wild. Over the years people have tried to domesticate zebras but most were unsuccessful. Upon reviewing the zebras' resumes it is evident that the zebra is best fit for the wild.

Like a zebra you will need to learn how to create a resume so that you can show you are the best fit for the job that you want. In this chapter I will show you a simple way to get it done correctly and quickly. You will also find additional resources here that I strongly urge you to look into for additional support.

When I was a sophomore, a friend told me about a restaurant that was hiring that offered good pay. I was excited about the opportunity, but when I found out that there was a resume involved, my excitement turned into fear. This was the first time I had to make a resume that really mattered for a job. I ended up consulting a resume-writing book for help, and I asked a mentor to review the resume I created. Because my resume was so well done, even though I'd never had actual experience working at a restaurant before, I ended up getting the job. Also, I got over my fear of creating a resume!

A resume is simply a list of a person's education, past jobs, and skills. This list is written and formatted in a certain way for it to qualify as a resume. When you apply for a job, you give it to the employer so they can get a general understanding of your background. It is like a report card that you hand over to your parents to see if you qualify for the gift you have been asking for for a long time. It is like SAT or ACT scores that colleges use to get a general idea of your skill levels in certain subjects. Your resume gives an employer a snapshot of your life as it relates to your work experience and education. They use the resume to decide if they should take the time to bring you in for an interview.

As a high school student it may seem like a daunting task to write a resume when you may have never worked an official job, but you actually have many qualifications that you may not have considered. For example, you can include informal work, such as babysitting, house or dog sitting, and mowing lawns. You can include any clubs, groups, or sports you have done regularly. Better yet, if you do everything in this book, you will have more quality experiences to add to your resume that will give you a leg up over anyone else applying for the job.

You don't have to reinvent the wheel when it comes to writing a resume. You can search for other high school student resumes as examples to see what you could include and how to set it up (formatting). The website thebalance.com offers fabulous information and lots of examples relevant to high school students.

You can also find templates that allow you to simply fill in information, and then the template does all the formatting so that the final resume looks neat, clean, and appropriately organized.

Microsoft Word has resume templates for beginners. To find it go to "File," "New," and then scroll down to "Resume and Cover Letters." If you are good with Word and/or graphic design, think about making your own resume template as a way to show off your skills. If you save it to Google Drive, you can access and edit it from any computer with Microsoft Word and internet access. Another option for a resume template is to do a Google search to find online options.

*Super Standout Zebra Tip*—keep your resume short, only one page total. Employers will love you for it because they are typically handling hundreds of applicants and resumes for a single position. The one-page resume stands out because it is clear, concise, and reader-friendly. Keep it to only one page by including formal or informal work experience, education, and attributes. Exclude any skills, past jobs, clubs, attributes, etc., that don't seem relevant to the particular job you are applying for.

Your future in terms of getting important internships and jobs depends on how well you can craft a resume, so the earlier you can get started learning this skill, the better. In addition to following my advice, bring your resume to your school counselor, favorite teacher, or other qualified adult, and ask them to edit it, mark it up, so that it can be made even better.

## Zebra Action Time

1. Write a list of all of your past work experiences. It can be formal or informal.

2. Write a list of all of your educational experiences and attitude attributes.

3. Start creating a resume. Use a template to help you out. Proofread it and then get someone else to proofread it too.

4. Think of a specific job that you desire to work at, and see if your resume would fit for that position. One way that you can do this is by removing the parts that are irrelevant to the position and focusing only on what's relevant to it. You also want to make sure that it's one page only.

5. After you've proofread it three times, send it or print it and deliver it to an adult to get their editing ideas. Make those revisions.

6. Send it out to a company you are interested in working for—and see what happens!

## Up Next

Making a resume presents you on paper, but the clothes you wear introduces you in person. Try on a new suit or dress to succeed like a zebra.

# CHAPTER 26

# *Try On a Nice Suit or Dress*

*You can have anything you want in life if you dress for it.*

—Edith Head

A S A NEWBORN a zebra foal has brown and white stripes. It is when it grows older that the colors change to black and white stripes. Zebra's skin serves as their clothing. The colors of their coat keep them cool in the hot African savannah. The coat also makes them quite distinctive to us humans. After all, you can always tell a zebra by its stripes!

Your appearance says a lot about you. The way that you dress, what you wear, and how you speak communicate volumes to the world about how you want to be perceived. Dressing for success both puts you in the mindset to better achieve that success and puts others in the mindset that you have already achieved that success. Even though it is about appearance—what you wear—it affects your own and others' mindsets about you. It's amazing. Dressing like the person that you want to be puts you in a better position to become that person; you will begin to see the results of that type of person that you desire to be. If your goal is to be an A student, you want to think, act, and look like an A student.

Don't dress like a suspect; dress like a prospect. The way you dress draws attention to you. People will determine whether or not they should listen to you based on what you are wearing. For example, if we were meeting for the first time and you noticed that my teeth were not brushed, my shirt buttoned incorrectly, my pants covered in grease stains, and my shoes had holes in them, what would your perception be? Would you listen to my advice on how to become a success? Would you invite me to speak at your school? Most likely, it would be no because my appearance doesn't match with the message.

The effect of clothing on attitude and professional success is quite interesting. Research shows that what you wear affects your behavior. Wearing business attire puts you in a professional frame of mind. Also, first impressions are very important, and clothes make up a large part of a first impression. So, it only makes sense to work this to your advantage.

I encourage you to experience this phenomenon yourself. You can go to a store to experience the internal changes that come along with a change of clothes. Go to a major store and try on a complete outfit. Look in the mirror. Take a picture of yourself. Notice how you look and how you feel because you look that way. Another idea is to ask an adult who is a similar size to you if you can try on one of their professional outfits. Then do the same—look in the mirror and take a selfie. Reflect on how you look and feel.

## Zebra-Trail-to-Success: The What

Young men: you want to get a collared button-down shirt for most jobs. On occasion if you are still in high school, then short sleeves are fine.

Second, get khaki pants. Third, a polo shirt. Fourth, a dress shoe in a neutral color, such as black or brown. Five, a neutral-colored belt. Six, a sweater to layer over a collared button-down.

Young ladies: you should get a polo shirt, khaki pants, a skirt, knee-length or longer, a collared button-down shirt, a sweater to wear by itself or layered over a collared button-down, a blouse, and a tailored dress. Your shoes should be flats or low heels in a neutral color. Those are some of the things that you want to get to dress for success.

When Leon was applying for his first job as a sales representative for Tupperware, he had never worn a suit before. So he went to the mall to check out a few men's clothing stores and found a navy blue suit and white dress shirt with a red tie. He tried on the whole set and felt like a million dollars. He had never seen himself in a suit before. He felt like he could achieve all of his dreams. Leon asked his parents to pitch in so that he could purchase the suit. The rest is history: he went to the interview with a bounce in his step. The interviewer sensed something special about this particular interview compared to previous ones. Leon answered the questions with confidence and got the job on the spot.

## More Resources

Do an image search for "high school interview outfits" to get some ideas for a complete look.

At the site work.chron.com, you can find great tips on how to dress professionally on a budget.

Many nonprofit organizations aimed at helping people find and keep jobs offer professional attire to borrow, in addition to job training and interview preparation help. Dressforsuccess.org is an international organization aimed at helping women gain financial independence. The Alliance of Career Development Non-Profits, which is at the site acdnonline.org, helps people enter or reenter the workforce. It's possible these organizations can help you acquire professional clothing.

Zebras dress the way they want to be addressed. You can too. You can dress for success. Try on a new suit or dress this week, and make the moves to build a wardrobe of professional attire.

## Zebra Action Time

1. What does success looks like in terms of attire for you?

2. How do the top people in the field or job you are applying for dress? Model after them.

3. Save up or ask for a sponsor to buy at least one new professional outfit in the next month or so.

4. When you are trying on the new outfit, ask your family, friends, and strangers for their initial impression to see if the outfit is conveying the right message.

5. Try to make a goal to add three to five different professional pieces of clothing to your closet this year.

## Up Next

Dressing for success will take care of the cover. Now let's work on the inside to get you ready to master the interview.

# CHAPTER 27

## *Master the Interview*

*Success doesn't come to you, you go to it.*

—Marva Collins

ZEBRAS HAVE TO learn how to "master interviews" to land important roles in their dazzle. Zebra interviews consist of physical feats: running, fighting, circling, and sighting. The zebras that succeed at these tests don't simply hope everything falls into place. They practice. They train. Similarly, you'll have to prepare for job interviews so that you can prove yourself and land the roles you want, both in part-time work and in your greater career.

As you'll recall from the chapter on resumes, I created my first resume to get a job at a restaurant. Because my resume was good, the restaurant didn't simply hire me; they called me for an interview. That was my first job interview, and I was quite nervous. The interviewer asked me questions about my resume and the job application. Lucky for me, I had prepared for almost any question days before the actual interview. My nervousness wasn't due to lack of preparation but due to the new experience. I ended up getting hired, and the rest is history. Takeaways from my first interview: 1) I was nervous, and that's normal. 2) I made sure to prepare beforehand, and that prep was key in my landing that job.

In this chapter I'm going to share a proven strategy for mastering the art of the interview. You will never feel unprepared for an interview. You will stand out like a zebra in a herd of horses.

First impressions are very important. To make a great first impression at the interview be certain to put into practice the many lessons from this book. First, you should arrive before the interview is scheduled to start. If something goes wrong and you predict you will be late, then you should contact the interviewer and let them know.

Next, you should be wearing professional attire, and you should practice the art of engaged listening during the interview. Review that chapter to recall the importance of making eye contact and sitting and standing with good posture. Remember, your intention and people's perception may not be the same. Strive to make them match. Remember, everything counts, whether we like it or not! Make sure your outfit, body language, and grooming are all professional. Before the actual interview, while you wait in a reception area or lobby, make sure you are behaving professionally there too.

It's crucial that you bring the right tools. Bring your resume, a list of references, a notebook of your own, and a pen too. Record questions you want to ask the interviewer in this notebook as well. Don't assume you'll remember the questions either because it's easy to forget things when on the spot. Take the effort to write them down beforehand. The interviewer will notice as well. Take notes during the interview too. This also suggests to the interviewer that you are responsible and professional. If it's applicable, bring a portfolio of a sample of your work. Make sure you spend time on searching for and purchasing a high quality portfolio, including paper.

Beforehand practice interviewing with an adult. Practice with family. There are fairly standard questions, and even strange ones, that people ask in interviews. You can find all that online. Practicing will help boost your confidence and preparedness. When the day comes, you will walk in with a hop in your step, which in turn will make a better impression.

Do research on the place you are applying to work for. Interviewers will be impressed if you already know important information about the company. They will be negatively impressed if it shows that you know very little. Stand out in the right way!

Another point about your attire: dress according to the job that you are applying for. For more "casual" type jobs, like working at a fast-food restaurant or as a cashier at a grocery, dress in business casual attire, like khaki pants or a skirt, and a polo shirt. For fancier places, like a sit-down restaurant or a help desk position, dress in professional attire, like khaki pants or a skirt, a long-sleeved button-down shirt, and a sweater. Dress accordingly.

No matter how the interview went (or how you think it went), send a thank-you note afterwards to the interviewer. You can also send an email, but a handwritten note makes a greater impression. I'm always moved when I receive handwritten thank-you notes. There is usually a seven-day window for sending the note. I usually carry with me thank-you cards with stamped envelopes so that I can send notes out faster. Most people won't do that. It gives you an edge over the competition.

I remember Lisa, who was a sophomore, who had an interview for office work. She prepared by researching about the real estate company and reviewing possible questions that the interviewer might ask her. She went into the interview with confidence knowing she had prepared. The interviewer was impressed with what Lisa knew about the company and its founders and how she could fit in with her skillset.

The site slideshare.net offers some great advice for interviewing well. Here's a snapshot of some of their recommendations:

- Arrive 15 minutes early.

- Have on hand at least one extra copy of your resume, even if you've already sent the place a copy.

- Know the names of the people you meet, and use their names when you speak to them.

- Bring a notebook and pen, and take notes.

- Give a firm handshake and maintain regular eye contact during the interview.

- Smile!

Use the information in this chapter as a launching pad and not a seat. Use the tips here to help with your interviewing prep, but also do added research on your own to understand the art and skill of interviewing, and then master it!

## Zebra Action Time

1. What are your three biggest takeaways from this chapter?

2. Make a checklist of the action items in this chapter.

3. Search for interview questions online to add to your list.

4. When do you plan to start practicing and with whom? How often do you plan to practice? Remember, perfect practice makes permanent.

5. Practice greeting and smiling in the mirror daily. Look for ways to be more friendly, sincere, and warm in your greetings. You can also practice giving firm handshakes with eye contact. You can practice with your siblings, friends, or parents. Practice, and in due time you will become a pro.

## Up Next

Mastering the interview will allow you to be in a best position to get the job. Getting the job is what we'll address in the coming chapter.

# CHAPTER 28

## *Get a Job*

*Choose a job you love, and you will
never have to work a day in your life.*

—Confucius

AFTER A CERTAIN period of time, a foal, a baby zebra, grows up
and learns how to fend for itself. It learns its job to keep up with
the dazzle. In fact, it has just a few minutes to understand the job of
keeping up with its mother and the dazzle as they move to graze or escape
from a predator.

Just like for the zebra, there comes a time in your life when you must take
on adult roles. I recommend doing that in high school by taking on a part-
time job. It's a great way to get your foot in the adult world.

One of my earliest jobs was working at my parents' insurance agency. I did
clerical work like filing papers and data entry where I would type the
customer's contact information into our customer management program. I
was earning about $100 a week. At first, honestly I was doing it just for the
money. I remember how earning my own money made me feel

independent. It was freedom not to have to ask my parents for money and approval to buy a new pair of shoes, for example.

Later I realized that there were many more benefits to doing the part-time work. For instance, I learned to balance school and work. It was hard because I was working 15 hours each week and also going to school, but I learned to decrease my time watching TV and increase my time studying and working. Also, I was able to add this work experience onto my college applications and resume. To pay my way through college, I even continued working at my parents' insurance agency. It was a great way to get introduced to the work world without the huge commitment full-time work would require of me.

You too can enjoy all these benefits when you start working after school or on weekends. Also, working part-time while in high school provides helpful experience and insight for those who plan to enter the workforce right after high school or work while attending college to support themselves and/or pay tuition.

To find jobs, I recommend starting your search by asking adults in your community—your parents, extended family, teachers, coaches, etc.—if they know of any business looking for workers. Also, inquire at the businesses you frequent. Even if they don't have a sign posted or postings online, at your favorite coffee shop, restaurant, or clothing store, the turnover is frequent, and they could suddenly be in need of a new worker. Make sure you already have all of your contact info written neatly on a piece of paper that you can hand over to them and that you are appropriately attired when you inquire in person at these establishments.

Be sure to look online as well. The site livecareer.com has a list of teen jobs and additional resources for finding, applying to, and interviewing for jobs. You can also visit indeed.com, which is a simple, user-friendly, no-clutter website that helps you search for jobs. Monster.com is also a great job search tool with additional resources.

## Zebra-Trail-to-Success for Landing the Job

To actually land that job, we've covered some of the steps: the resume, the professional dress, and the interview. Let's discuss a few more.

*First*—be persistent. When you submit an application online or in person, within a few days follow up with a phone call (if possible) or an email in which you introduce yourself, share that you applied for a particular position (and the date you submitted the application), say that you are very interested and excited about it, and announce that you would love to talk more about how you can contribute to the business. Be persistent too by applying to many jobs. Don't get discouraged if you don't get called in for an interview because it is very competitive out there.

*Second*—clean up your online presence. Make sure all of your online pictures, videos, and statuses are sending the right message. It's been said, "What you post online lives forever." Beware of what you are posting on your social media pages.

Briana worked as a cashier at a Publix. Before she was hired, she had thought since no one had called or emailed that she may not get the job. Instead of waiting for the phone to ring, she called, emailed, and even stopped by the store. The store manager, who had interviewed her, remembered and was impressed that she was persistent. She got hired.

The great news is you can get hired too. Simply follow the steps outlined in this chapter as well as previous chapters, and you will get hired.

## Zebra Action Time

1. Prepare your resume. Save a copy in a folder on your desktop.

2. Use the job search tool on indeed.com, monster.com, and livecareer.com today to see what comes up.

3. Review the list of teen-related jobs on livecareer.com to see if you are interested in any.

4. Look for "Help Wanted" signs at stores and restaurants you frequent. Even if you don't see one, inquire anyway.

5. Ask your parents, friends, and teachers if they know of any job openings for teenagers. Take action and watch what happens.

## Up Next

Getting hired is one thing, but staying hired and getting promoted is another thing. Chapter 29 addresses learning to speak in public so that you can open up more opportunities for yourself at work and school.

# CHAPTER 29

## *Work On Public Speaking*

---

*Words have incredible power. They can make people's hearts soar, or they can make people's hearts sore.*

—Dr. Mardy Grothe

---

ZEBRAS SPEAK. SOME of the ways zebras communicate are barking, braying, snorting, or huffing to get their point across to their family group and to the whole dazzle. The most influential zebras are the ones who regularly communicate to the dazzle.

Public speaking is one of the most-feared things to do. In fact, I have heard that lots of people would rather lie dead in a coffin than give a speech. While I'm not sure how true that is, I do know many people would rather sit in the audience than be the one presenting. As a seasoned public speaker myself, I always tell people that the good news is that public speaking is a learnable skill. It will take time to develop just like any other skill, but you can do it. You can be a better speaker.

Before I go into some public-speaking basics, you need to realize there are many benefits to becoming an experienced public speaker. For one, when you are accustomed to speaking publically, then when you are faced with a group interview—meaning you must sit before a team of people in an interview—whether for a job, internship, scholarship, or college admissions, you are more prepared. It is a different experience conversing in one-on-one situations versus a one-on-four situation. Other benefits include a greater ability to speak on your feet, which can be helpful in certain job situations. You can expand your network when people hear your point of view; they may want to meet you or do business with you. You will boost your confidence. Speaking in public can give a jolt to your confidence when you do it well. You can gain publicity because public speaking is a great way to get your message to a wider audience.

Jeremiah, a junior, said this about his first public speaking experience:

*The first time I spoke publicly was in church for a youth night. I was really scared and my heart was beating rapidly. As I started speaking, I began to feel very comfortable and ended up speaking longer than I'd thought. What made me really like it was when many people were complimenting me on my speech and wanted me to do it again next time. That night really made me like public speaking. Even though I'm shy, I'm willing to try it again because it was really fun.*

## The Very Basics

First, let's make this clear: speaking in public is a means of communication. It is similar to writing an essay or researching a paper, but with an obvious difference: it is spoken. As with any form of communication, whether spoken or written, there must be a main message. What is the purpose of your speech? What point are you trying to make? What action do you want your listeners to take after hearing your presentation?

You don't just write an essay without first working on an outline or having some general idea of where you are heading. The same applies to a speech. What are the points that you want to make? What sub-points, examples, stories, stats, etc., do you have for each point? How will you close your talk? Think about what you want your listeners to do or reconsider after your presentation. Focus on that. Write out your closing and intro. And practice a lot—in front of a mirror, in front of family and friends, and in front of a camera. Watch a video of yourself and determine what you need to improve.

A good framework to use when crafting your speech is this: tell them what you are going to tell them, tell them, and then tell them what you have told them. It's that simple. There are more advanced ways of developing a speech, but this will take you a long way. Master this so that you can graduate to the more advanced techniques.

Learn how to communicate to a group so that you can be in a better position to succeed at school and in life. You have tremendous opportunities to work on the strategies mentioned here today. There are classes, clubs, and other extracurricular activities that you can take part in to upgrade your speaking. Roll up your sleeves and get ready to work on the action exercises.

## Zebra Action Time

1. What do you want to speak about? What points do you want to make?

2. Do a brain dump. Take a sheet of paper and write the topic on the top line. Then write down as many ideas, points, quotes, stories, and anything else that comes to mind on that topic. You can even do a mind map, whichever works for you.

3. Circle the three to five key points that you want to include in your talk. Look for supporting points to add under your main points.

4. Create an outline and add additional information to any places lacking. Then write out or talk out your speech. Practice and tweak it several times alone and with your family and friends. Ask for feedback and make the necessary changes.

5. Deliver your speech like a zebra. You can do this.

## Up Next

With public speaking, as with so many things in life, comes responsibility. In the next chapter we will cover the power of taking full responsibility for your life.

# CHAPTER 30

## *Take Full Responsibility*

*"You must take personal responsibility. You cannot change the circumstance, the seasons, or the wind, but you can change yourself. That is something you have charge of."*

—Jim Rohn

ZEBRAS IN MIGRATION will often cross crocodile-infested waters. A young stallion will have to fend off crocs by kicking while crossing. By taking full responsibility for the situation at hand, as opposed to just hoping for the best or being in denial, the zebra increases its chance of surviving the crossing.

Your life will only change when you take full responsibility for yourself and your life. Zebras take full responsibility. You can create the life that you desire by taking ownership of yourself, your words, your actions, and your choices.

Things will not change. Life will not change. Your grades will not change. Your relationships will not change—until you take ownership.

Too many people pass the buck. They blame society, the government, their parents, their school, etc., for where they are and where they are going. As a zebra, take charge of your life by taking responsibility. Realize you are in the driver's seat of your life—and drive.

You are not a puppet. People don't make you do things. You are not a robot configured to do what others want you to do. You are a human being. A powerful human being. When you take responsibility, you take back control of your life. You boost your own self-esteem. You feel more confident and in control. There are times you will face situations that are out of your control. Those should not be the focus of your attention. Focus only on what you can control even in those out-of-control moments.

I can remember a time years ago when I was a teen working at my parents' insurance office. A wealthy man in a gold Rolls Royce came in and wanted to purchase insurance. After he had signed the application, I went outside to take photos of his pristine car. He asked me, "What do you want to do with your life?" I told him that I was living for the moment and wasn't sure what I wanted to do. He responded, "You have to have a plan and take ownership to make progress in your life." His words struck me. Progress occurs when your actions, decisions, and results are your own. It occurs when you know that you are responsible.

Clark never had much growing up, and he knew that if he wanted to go to college he would have to take it upon himself to prepare financially. In his tenth grade year Clark found a pre-collegiate program at Florida International University that would help him prepare for the college experience as well as providing a plethora of scholarship opportunities. While most students were at home in their beds, Clark was in a library studying for the ACT and SAT, and applying for every scholarship he could find. What finally happened to Clark? He graduated, passed his SAT and ACT with high scores, and had five different scholarships that covered all his college expenses. Clark took responsibility for himself, his circumstances, and where he wanted to go in life. By doing so, he created several options for himself.

To get back the control of your life repeat this phrase several times during the day: "I am responsible for my life, my feelings, and for every result I get." Whenever I feel the pressure of passing the buck, I repeat the affirmation and get my power back. You can do the same.

Be careful to only take responsibility for what's in your power. Perhaps your parents recently got divorced, and you are now blaming yourself for it. It was not in your power to keep their marriage intact. If you continue blaming yourself or taking responsibility for that which is out of your control, you will impede your success. It's like driving a car with the emergency brake on. It slows you down. It adds unnecessary stress. You don't need to add wood to the fire. Only take ownership for what you can control—your attitude, your words, your actions (or inactions), and your responses.

When you take full responsibility for your life—both for the great things and the less-than great things you say, do, think, etc., then you empower yourself. You put yourself in charge of your life. It's a glorious feeling. You have the power in your hands. When you don't own your own life and fail to take responsibility for yourself, you will be powerless. If you are powerless, you will turn into a puppet, a robot, or a whiner. It's your life. It's your future. Take responsibility, and you will succeed like a zebra.

## Zebra Action Time

1. How do you plan on taking full responsibility?

2. When was the last time you blamed someone else for your life?

3. What does it mean to take responsibility for whatever is in your power to control?

## Up Next

Now it's time you dash to the finish line to earn your stripes.

# CHAPTER 31

## *Earn Your Stripes*

---

*You don't have to be great to start,*
*but you have to start to be great.*

—Zig Ziglar

---

THE END OF this book is the beginning of something special: you are now well on your way to succeeding like a zebra. By implementing any and all of these 30 proven strategies today while you are in high school, you will set yourself up for a life of more options, opportunities, and overall success. You are giving yourself that certain edge, so you can leap higher, farther, and more vibrantly than most of your peers. By employing these strategies, you will revolutionize your life. You will earn your stripes. This can be the turning point for you.

The four sections:

Make a Plan. Plan for your future, so you don't fail your present and future. Plan now. Plan today. Start by keeping a journal, and move on from there. Join the zebras that are leading the group, not the ones trailing so far behind that they get lost.

Gain Knowledge. Knowledge is power. Right? Sort of, but not exactly. Knowledge in itself has dormant power. It's like a fully charged battery that isn't being used. Knowledge becomes powerful when it is applied properly. In this section we covered several key skills you need to know and master while in high school to succeed in college and life.

Build Character. Your talent and skills will take you only as far as your character will keep you. Character is the part of you that is not seen but is felt. It is the foundation of the house. It is that part of you that is below the surface that holds everything else in place in your life. Zebras are people of strong character. Continue to build good character in your life, and you will go higher and farther.

Prepare for the Future. Life after high school will be starkly different. You will have more responsibilities. Ready yourself now so that you have more and better options than your peers who are just drifting along, refusing to address the reality of the impending future. The future belongs to the zebras who prepare for it.

In order for the strategies in this book to work for you, you have to work the strategies. Not just once but as long as it takes to see the results you desire. Zebras push hard. Zebras take action. Take action today! Earn those stripes!

For readers seeking to take it to the next level, I've developed a special bonus section. Simply send me an email at hello@nickzizi.com and say, "I want in." I will send you bonus resources that will inspire, motivate, and educate you on your zebra trail to success. I want to help you succeed like a zebra. I want to help accelerate your success. Let's do this.

# Acknowledgments

This book, like everything else I have created in my life, is the result of a huge team effort. I extend my deepest gratitude and thanks to the following:

To my lovely wife, Sherline Zizi, and my five little zebras, Zach, Bri, Izzy, Eli, and Grace—you all allowed me to work on this project during the late evenings and early mornings, while you kids were up doing what little zebras do. Thank you for your endless support. Love you.

To my parents whose support means the world to me.

To my sisters, Deborah and Daphne—you are the best beta readers and sisters in the world.

To Jonathan Laurince, my mastermind buddy, who continues to stretch me.

To Jonathan Sprinkles, my business coach, who dropped some sprinkles on my brand.

To my wonderful editor, Nancy, for ironing out the rough edges and turning this book into what it is today.

To WHOP and WHOPA for your continued support.

To Team Zebra Guerdiana, Chrisla, Kenny, Jeff, Wills, Anichard, Marsha, Terry, Michelle, Nancy, Rebecca, Robert, Markesner, Samuel, for your story contributions and support.

To Chandler, Scott, and Sean for your guidance and support.

To the Succeed Like A Zebra Book Launch Team for helping extend the reach of this new book.

Thank you.

# About the Author

Nick "The Zebra" Zizi is a student leadership speaker and TEDx presenter who delivers messages on student achievement and student leadership at conferences, schools, and other events. He is the author of two other books, *Multiple Streams of Motivation: How Motivation Can Change Your Life* and *30 Ways to Ace School and Life*. He is also a radio personality in a weekly broadcast geared towards developing student leaders.

As the founder of the Nick Zizi Scholarship, Nick and his organization have given over $10,000 in scholarship money to deserving high school seniors.

He is the husband of Sherline, and they both have five little zebras.

# WHO ELSE WANTS TO
# SUCCEED LIKE A ZEBRA?!

*Nick Zizi's high-energy, fun, content-filled and interactive style teaches students how to lead and succeed first on campus then in life.*

## HOW TO USE NICK ZIZI

1. SCHOOL ASSEMBLIES
2. LEADERSHIP CONFERENCES
3. ORIENTATION AND WELCOME-BACK PROGRAMS
4. CAREER FAIRS FOR STUDENTS
5. GRADUATION AND COMMENCEMENT PROGRAMS
6. EDUCATOR WORKSHOPS OR TRAINING

**When Results Matter Nick Zizi is the speaker you want for your next event.**

**His fun and engaging style keeps his audiences on the edge of their seats as he shares Z-Rated content that enables them to go from Z to A.**

**Here's what others have said about Nick's Presentations:**

*"Our students were high fiving each other, taking notes and fully engaged in his presentations. We have three words to describe Nick and his presentations.. 'Inspirational, Informative and Leadership Driven!'"*

**- Sonya Russell, M.Ed**
FL BPA State Advisor

*"Our students were so moved that many of them wrote letters expressing their gratitude and what they plan on changing as a result of hearing Nick Zizi's message."*

**-Ms. Deette Naukana**
Principal

*"He has an uncanny ability to connect with students while providing great content..."*

**- Simone Shaker**
Activities Director, New York

## DATES ARE LIMITED. REQUEST NICK ZIZI FOR YOUR NEXT EVENT TODAY!
## WWW.NICKZIZI.COM

NICK ZIZI
UNLEASH YOUR ZEBRA ®

Made in the USA
Columbia, SC
12 March 2019